Endorsements

"One man's journey from heartbreak to healing told in a personal, conversational style. You get the feeling you are reading an unfiltered private diary. This book does not pretend to be a piece of great literature. But if you want to look through an open window into the heart and soul of a man trying to come to terms with loss, this book is perfect for you. Each of us will, in time, have to cross many of the same bridges the author has crossed in this book. He seems to know this and is gentle with the reader. I appreciated the book and found it to be an easy read covering a topic that has no easy parts."

~ **Rev. Bob Luckin, DD**

"Mike Russell reminds us that when we feel torn apart, due to the death of a loved one or friend, we must go through the various stages of grief. Through his experiences, insights, humor, connection to his beloved wife, Barb who died, and his poetry he weaves together a tapestry of love, truth, wisdom, and healing. This is a must-read for all who are grieving."

Sharon Lund, Author of

Sacred Living, Sacred Dying: A Guide to Embracing Life and Death

"The lesson to be learned from *My Compass, Our Story* is that if you do not bring forth what is within you it will destroy you but if you bring forth what is within you it will save you. Read on and prepare yourself for life."

~ **Bernie Siegel, MD,** Author of

A Book of Miracles and Love, Animals & Miracles

"This *is* an important book. And not just for men, either. As I read, I saw that so much of the book's wisdom also applies to women who find themselves in grief and not fully functioning. Further, I felt the book's contents would be useful even if the adult who had passed was not a spouse but a parent, or a brother or sister.

"I found the poetry interspersed throughout to be beautiful and thought provoking; a pleasant surprise, considering I don't normally choose to read poetry!

"In short, *My Compass, Our Story* is a worthy and valuable addition to adults grieving the loss of another adult."

~ **Lynette M. Smith,** Author of

How to Write Heartfelt Letters to Treasure

Endorsements

"Mike Russell's writing is brave, authentic, inspired, descriptive, and peppered with sage advice for anyone healing from the loss a loved one. His lessons are insightful, wise, and touching."

~ Rev. Judy Winkler, president

New View New Life (a prison ministry)

MY COMPASS, OUR STORY

MY COMPASS, OUR STORY

A Journey Through Death and Life

Mike Russell

My Compass, Our Story

A Journey Through Death and Life

Copyright © 2017 Mike Russell

All rights reserved. No part of this book may be used or reproduced by any means, graphic, electronic, or mechanical, including photocopying, recording, taping, or by any information storage retrieval system without the written permission of the publisher except in the case of brief quotations embodied in critical articles and reviews.

ISBN: 978-0-9896593-8-3
ISBN: 0-9896593-8-0
Library of Congress Control Number: 2017930619

Cover Design: LincMedia Design

Sacred Life Publishers™
SacredLife.com
Printed in the United States of America

Contents

Endorsements i

Dedication xv

Foreword by Steve Arndt xvii

Introduction—My Compass xxi

Chapter 1—First Steps 1
      Poems
 Inspired 3
 You Are 5
 The Compass 7
 I Found God Within 9
 Finding Love 12
 Two Souls 14
 Theme Song 16
 Walking Backwards 18

Chapter 2—Men Don't Cry 19
      Poems
 Stop-Sign Tears 20
 Second Guesses 22
 Quiet Peace 25
 Where Are You? 27

Chapter 3 — Tackling Yourself 29
Poems
Tackling Ghosts 31
Slow Treadmill 33
A Need to Be Sad 35

Chapter 4 — The New Normality 37
Poems
Freedom 39
The Leaf 41
Life and Death 43
Hope 45
Leaving 48

Chapter 5 — The Dreaded Question 49
Poems
Direct Connect 51
The Veil 53
The Path 56

Chapter 6 — The Silence 57
Poems
What Now? 59
Softly 62
Long and Short 65
A Day in Time 67
To Remember 70

Chapter 7 — Unexpected Strength 71
Poems
Silence 74

Contents

Some Days 77
Catharsis 81
Talk to the Wind 84

Chapter 8 — Different but All the Same 85
Poems

The Puzzle of Life 88
Does It Matter? 91
Purpose 94

Chapter 9 — Bravery 95
Poems

You Tried to Tell Me 97
Live 101

Chapter 10 — Out of the Cave 103
Poems

Spirit 105
So Much Time 108
Remember 111

Chapter 11 — Into the Parade 113
Poems

One Step 116
Being at Peace 119

Chapter 12 — Unexpected Paths 121
Poems

Peace Blanket 124
Companion 127
The Burden 129

Scents 132

Chapter 13 — Taking Stock 133
Poems
The Gift 138
Eternally 140
Peace 142

Chapter 14 — Surviving the Twists and Turns 143
Poems
Thank You 145
Searching for Peace 148
Lights 151
Another Time 153

Chapter 15 — The "Voice of Reason" 155
Poems
Words 157
The Trip 160
Street Corner Sobriety 162
You Are with Me 165

Chapter 16 — Those Little Moments 167
Poems
Transformation 169
Synchronicity 172
Eagle 175
Past and Future 178

Contents

Chapter 17 — Connecting and Reflecting 179
Poems
Mist 181
Happiness 184
Being Lost 186
Weight 188
You Know Someone Loves You 190

Chapter 18 — The End and the Beginning 191

Quote 199

Acknowledgments 201

About the Author 205

I would like to dedicate this book to the memory of Barbara Grace Russell, whose soul purpose was to create a nuclear family through which she could use her talents of organization, encouragement, and direction. Her love resides within all her family and will extend out through the generations. She was there for me when I needed it most, and through her spiritual communication, she helped lead me out of the fog of grief. Thank you, my loving friend and partner.

Foreword

My relationship with Mike Russell began more than thirty-five years ago, in the small community of Mt. Angel, Oregon. Mike was an up-and-coming banker, and I was the principal of the local grade school. Our families met and immediately began an enduring friendship that has spanned years of career moves, family additions, and life altering changes, including the death of a child and a spouse. Each of us deals with hard times in different ways, and Mike is no different. The book that Mike has written focuses on his spiritual, mental, and physical journey, and how he navigated life's route, which was completely re-coursed after the January 2009 death of his wife, Barbara. He hopes people can use his book to assist them in their own life journey, especially when that passage suddenly takes an unwanted turn.

December is usually the time when people make resolutions based on what took place the prior year. I am sure at Christmas in 2008 Mike was busily formulating resolutions that focused on his family and his work, the wild and crazy mortgage market. According to the *New York Times*, the following were top five New Year's resolutions that year:

1. Spend more time with family
2. Lose weight
3. Get fit
4. Quit a bad habit
5. Enjoy life more

December turned into January, and his 2009 resolutions were dashed with the unexpected death of his wife. Nowhere on the list was "Deal with the death of a spouse" or "Nurture six young adult children on one's own"—both daunting scenarios made exponentially worse when working in tandem. Instead of focusing on resolutions, Mike was forced to face the stark reality that his wife, the mother of their children and the rock of their relationship, would no longer be the person he had been awakening beside each morning. While the rest of the world (or so it probably seemed to Mike) was trying to figure out how to spend more time with family, shed those few pounds, and find new ways to enjoy life, Mike was thrust into the unenviable position of widower, making him the sole decision maker, caretaker of teens still at home, nurturer of other young adult children, and breadwinner. Mike had little time for himself and for dealing with his own feelings, as the immediate needs and care of his family were more pressing.

Life does not come with an instruction book to see us through turmoil and crises. No amount of college courses taken for degree completion prepares a person for challenges faced when grave misfortune strikes. Mike has written this book to share his journey, in hopes that others can learn from his experiences. Yet he admits that no two people grieve the same way or at the same pace. In the Five Stages of Grief, it states people must go through the following steps when dealing with a life-changing event:

1. Denial
2. Anger
3. Bargaining
4. Depression
5. Acceptance

Mike writes that it took him almost five years to get through these stages—more years than many, yet fewer than some. Mike has a unique way of blending prose with poetry and uses life examples to illustrate how he learned to cope with the death of a spouse, regroup, and eventually recover. After coming to accept the hand put before him, with help of a spiritual angel, Mike has since embarked on a new path.

The journey to publish this guidebook began as a blog—a personal and therapeutic release for Mike. As the months passed, he slowly transitioned through the stages of grief, and the blog morphed into this book. It does not tell you how to survive a crisis; rather, it speaks to what he found as personal comfort and solace during his walk through this dark period. Mike knows the book is not intended to remove the difficult or bleak episodes from our lives but rather shed light on seeking a new and brighter tomorrow.

Mike Russell speaks from the depths of his soul, offers heart-wrenching lexis, and gives comfort to his readers. Read the words and take from them what you will and what you need. Good luck in your personal journey, and may you find peace and comfort by using and internalizing what Mike has written.

Steve Arndt, author of
Roads Less Traveled in Oregon
Retired Senior Associate Professor, *Warner Pacific College*

Introduction

My Compass

Barbara Grace Russell was my compass and my guide. I knew it the first time I met her. Barb was the love of my life for thirty-four years. We did pretty much everything together. After she fell ill, I became so caught up in the day-to-day, downward physical deterioration of her body that I did not truly acknowledge the reality of what was happening. I was unaware of how close her death really was. I cannot say that if I had taken my head out of the sand, I would have been able to change anything; but I do look back with sadness and some guilt. We tend to think that, had we known, we could have changed something to create a different outcome. Reality tells us differently. No matter how much we love someone, it is easy to get stuck in the rut of life and to follow the direction you have been pointed in while hoping for the best.

* * *

Death is so final and complicated in its emotional impact on a person.

Remembering back to the day she died is like a brilliant flash of light. Barb died of a massive heart attack brought on by complications from Type 2 diabetes. To me, diabetes is a very destructive, heat-seeking missile. It weakens the body into submission. Even though Barb had been diagnosed only a couple of years before her death, she was already following most of the prescribed medical regimen for patients with the condition. There were so many pills for so many things going wrong in her body that when I look back on it, I realize she didn't have a chance. You know the old saying, "Damned if you do, and damned if you don't." She knew where it was headed more than any of us did. After all, she was a retired nurse with a lot of knowledge in this area.

Back in 1975, we were both working at the Arizona Children's Hospital. One day I looked up from a desk where I was working as a ward clerk and saw a petite blonde with beautiful eyes staring me in the face. She asked me how old I was. One simple question. After my reply, she turned around and walked away. I laughed out loud after I got over the surprise. It turns out she had been put up to it as a bet by one of the other nurses. And that was it. I was hooked. Right then and there, I forgot about getting dumped by another girl and ended up falling hard for this nurse. I was only twenty years old. We married the following year and spent the next thirty-plus years creating a large family, mostly while living in Oregon.

    I think it would help for you to know Barb better. She was the ultimate mother. Motherhood was what her soul strived for. We had seven children. Our first son died at ten days old from a heart problem, and I think that event sent us on the large family route. Honestly, we never thought we would have more than two kids. It's kind of funny what happens along life's journey. I spoke at Barb's funeral about how she would have been mortified to have so many people make a fuss of her. At the same time she would have been so pleased by all the love shown by those in attendance.

    My wife was a kind and gentle woman who loved me and our children without exception, no matter what we did. She coached us all in her unique, encouraging way. Barb knew all our personalities and worked within each of our quirks to help make us who we are today. Don't get me wrong. Perfection is not what I am alluding to here. What I am saying is that Barb was most comfortable in her role as a mother, even though it drove her crazy at times. She was very good at motherhood.

I, on the other hand, can only admire her because I definitely do not excel at being the mom now that she is gone. However, I have had to learn to take on the role. Let me tell you, it has a very steep learning curve. What a person can take for granted in someone until he or she isn't around anymore is amazing, and you think, "Oh my God. How am I supposed to pull this off?" Hopefully, this helps explain who Barb was and why I would expect nothing else than for her to continue to guide me as my compass.

This book is about the journey I have been on since Barb died. It is about my highs and lows, my successes and failures, the connections, and the letting go. I really do not think this text could have been written without the strong bond between Barb and me. The interwoven connections we had through our life together have made possible all the things that have happened since her death. Existing in total grief is all-consuming.

Right after Barb's funeral, I felt a need to get to our favorite beach in Manzanita, Oregon. I went with my two daughters and one of their friends. I was in a complete fetal position in the front passenger seat listening to John Denver. You would have to know our family to realize that because Barb and I were always John Denver fans, we inspired the kids to be the same. The group of sad travelers headed to a favorite restaurant along the Oregon coast.

Introduction—My Compass

We had beautiful weather, but all the while I was being spiritually driven to get to our coast house in Nehalem. I needed to be by myself on the beach in Manzanita. To be driven to do anything at the time seemed odd. I certainly was not functioning at any level that could be considered normal. However, I could not get it out of my head that I had to be on that beach as soon as possible. I remember pushing the group north along the coast and telling them I was going to drop them off at the house and head to the beach alone.

It is hard to make clear what a powerful pull was being placed on me to get to Manzanita beach at that time. I could feel nothing. I was completely numb. My eyes were swollen from crying beyond what I thought was a rational amount of time. It is surprising I was able to drive myself there, given that I had no sense of awareness about me. When I got out of the car, I immediately and intuitively headed to the north end of the beach. I remember standing at the shore's edge and being devoid of any kind of emotion or strength within my body. Then I let loose tears I didn't think I had in me anymore. Without warning, I became angry. I know it is one of the stages of grief, but I think over the next hour, I went through every stage of grief simultaneously.

Basically, I let Barb have it for leaving me so suddenly. How could she leave me after we had shared such a genuine connection over the last thirty-four years? If you knew me, you would know I do not usually get angry. I heard Barb tell a friend one day that you could count on one hand the number of times I had truly been angry in our marriage. Well, this was one of those times. I remember looking around, and although there were a few people nearby on the beach, I seemed to be invisible to those people who were enjoying the beach. I looked at one woman, and it was like she was looking up the beach and straight through me. I ranted and raved. I finally demanded in a voice I did not recognize that I could not do this without her. I told Barb she had to continue to be with me and communicate with me because I was not going to be able to go on without her. As if that weren't enough, I then demanded she show me that she was listening. Until that point, I had looked around the beach and not seen anything on the sand— no shells, no rocks, nothing. I walked toward the end of the beach, and at that very moment, I noticed a sand dollar. I bent down and picked it up. And then another. And another.

Nothing had been in sight just moments before, and I said aloud, "If this is you, Barb, and this is your sign, you're going to need to give me nine shells." In my mind, nine was the number of people in our family; seven children and two parents. Right on cue, that is exactly what happened. As I walked and picked up these sand dollars, I had exactly nine in my hand. There were no other sand dollars on the beach. I started to relax, thinking Barb was listening, and I was embarrassed about my display of emotion.

I arrived at the rocks toward the end of the beach after putting all the sand dollars in my pocket. I felt some relief with these tokens. I took one step on a mossy boulder, and I remember my legs flying straight up in the air and coming down hard on the sand. Feeling clumsy, with my dignity nowhere to be found, I got to my feet and brushed the sand off myself. I seemed to be in one piece. It suddenly dawned on me that I had the sand dollars in my pocket. When I slid my hand in to feel them, I found they had shattered into dust. I laughed aloud, thinking Barb was playing a joke on me. After regaining my composure, I spoke to Barb again and told her that I understood her ironic humor. However, because I was a visual person, which she knew, she was going to have to provide me nine more sand dollars on my walk back down the beach. I was thinking, "That'll show her," because I already knew the stretch of beach I had just walked was completely barren.

I started hiking back, and almost immediately a sand dollar appeared in front of me, then another, and another. I had now collected eight more sand dollars that had appeared out of nowhere, but I was one short of nine. I asked Barb to give me a special one. Then the "Miracle of Manzanita" appeared in front of my right foot. I saw a sand dollar that had the complete carved picture of a figure in it.

To me it appeared as a perfectly carved picture of what I thought was Barb with her arms outstretched. I was suddenly not angry anymore. I very carefully picked up this miracle and cradled it in my hand. I was sure if I let it go, it would get hurt and no one would ever believe what had just happened. I immediately found a sizable log of driftwood, carefully laid out the sand dollars, and photographed them with my camera. Being a visual type of person and getting this kind of response from Barb allowed me to believe that she was listening to my pleas and really was going to help me through this struggle.

I made it back to the house and retold the story for my family many times. I was unable to get through it without becoming extremely emotional. Whenever I told this story, I would bring the special sand dollar out at the end and show it to anyone listening. Everyone else thought the final sand dollar looked like an angel outline. I can accept this interpretation because I now know Barb is my guardian angel and guide.

From that point on, the number nine became a very important number in my life; so much so, that when I see the number nine, it often means some form of communication with Barb is about to transpire. I would awaken at various times from sleep with thoughts involving some combination of the number nine. Sometimes I had to ignore it just to get some sleep.

Months went by as I walked and talked my way through my grief. In June 2009, on a long walk through downtown Hillsboro, Oregon, words started leaping into my head. No matter what I did, I could not get rid of or ignore them, so I made my way to a coffee shop, where I borrowed a pen, took a napkin, and wrote down the words. This was the first poem I ever wrote. The words hit me like a ton of bricks.

Poetry is definitely not my thing. I have never enjoyed poetry, written any, or really even liked to read it. But now, on these walks of mine, I was being flooded with words.

The poems would come in pieces or in complete form. At first, it was irritating. It then became a dutiful requirement for me to carry paper and pen on every stroll. I probably looked silly, walking around town while writing and not paying attention to where I was walking. Luckily, I tripped only a few times. Some days I would write ten poems on a five-mile walk, and others, I would be focused on one specific piece. I refer to this as a cosmic joke, knowing that Barb was the inspiration for what was coming through. I had asked for a continued connection and guidance, and I realized now that I might not have been specific enough. The joke was to give me poems to write down because it was well known that it was not my forte. I realized these poems were important, but I really did not know what to do with them. I kept putting them into a pile, thinking my job was done by simply writing them down for myself.

A close friend and I went to see the movie *Julie and Julia*. In the film is a screenshot of the blog site that she was using to communicate about her trip with Julia Child. I immediately thought I was supposed to use that medium in some way for these poems. After I got home and did some research, I created my blog. This was during September 2009. I figured I already had enough poems written to last a couple of years if I posted one a week. The same friend, who had seen the movie with me, suggested I write something about my journey in relation to losing Barb. At this point, I was listening to people and following signs that were in front of me. The first blog was created to change weekly and to include a journey entry that focused on what I was feeling that week.

It has evolved from a painful reminder to an enjoyable outlet, not only for what I feel and think but also as a way for me to communicate with other people who are grieving. Plenty of books tell a great deal about bereavement and grief. However, I believe the personal day-to-day experience of grief from a man's perspective is missing in our literature. I am a man with feelings, and I have been through a tremendously difficult and awe-inspiring time of my life. I am not ashamed of my feelings. I believe society puts too much pressure on us, particularly men, to bottle them up and move on.

Along this path, I have been inspired, I believe by my deceased wife, to write poetry about life and death, living and loving. I have no doubt about where this drive and content come from. To be honest, whether anyone else believes it really does not matter because faith transcends and allows me to continue on this journey. I have met some really wonderful people along the way who identify with the loss process. I have been given enough feedback to believe Barb and I are, indeed, on the right path and this project can help other people traveling down a road similar to mine. In addition to the poetry and blogs that were written during this period, I was also inspired to reach out and write a book about my best friend at the time, who was an intuitive and angelic energy practitioner.

Through our time together, I became acquainted with Archangel Raphael, who is channeled through Trisha Michael. Because of this growing interest and relationship with a need to seek another answer, I asked Archangel Raphael to provide input for this book in the hopes he would be able to provide a thread that would tie the timeframe and grief process together. The result was his direct quotes for each chapter, which provide a platform of what transpires in that timeframe. After I received these quotes, the thread provided turned out to be so simple that I had not recognized it at first.

He gives his input to weave love throughout the timeline of this book, by providing his special words to this human experience we all go through at one point or another. As with all of Archangel Raphael's messages, he shares love over and over again. I call this the "Thread of Love."

So what you end up with is an angelic quote, personal experiences that cover a period from death to life, and inspired poetry—all wrapped up in a ribbon. May the quotes of Archangel Rafael and the following love story—consisting of my prose contributions and the poetry Barb inspired—give you peace, and may you enter the light a new and renewed soul.

Chapter 1

First Steps

The journey begins with a crack of light in great darkness.
Shining light eternally forth allows darkness to remember
the embrace of Love.
~Archangel Raphael

Inspiration comes in many forms. You may be inspired to take a walk, build a backyard memorial, or write something. In my case, inspiration has allowed me to do all of these. My wife is my inspiration. Since her passing on January 29, 2009, I was inspired to write poetry. I am sure this has happened to other people, but if you knew me, it would come as a total surprise. I am going to be honest. I grew up not liking or reading poetry. So my writing poetry can be considered to be a kind of cosmic joke. I believe it is Barb's way of getting me outside of my comfort zone and ready to do other things.

I have never studied how to compose poetry, what is proper, or whether it is worth reading. What I can promise is these poems were all given to me with love and intention. The verses or titles flash in my mind and do not let go until I write them down. Once I do write them down, I typically forget them. I do not even remember them an hour later. I know they are coming from a source outside of me. I find this to be extremely comforting or scary depending on how I want to view it. I hope these poems will bring comfort where needed and, most of all, will show that love crosses all boundaries. Be open, be loved, and know you are not alone.

Inspired

She lit up my world,
directed my dreams,
and gave me love even
if I did not deserve it.

She came in peace,
and died with love,
sending us all on paths of our own.

She gave to everyone,
serving first,
receiving later.

The beam of light that she is now,
will change the world
for the better.

For me, when Barb died, it was like a light went out. I remember feeling like every cell in my body was drained of energy. I felt lifeless, non-emotional, cold, and hopeless, rather like the marionette that hung in my closet when I was a kid. My form was here, but nothing within me was working.

Chapter 1—First Steps

You Are

*You are my light
you are my soul
you are me.*

*You are right
you are wrong
you are me.*

*You are love
you are fear
you are me.*

*You are my light
you are my soul
you are me.*

In the early days following Barb's death, simple things like walking were difficult. I tried walking around one block and could hardly move my legs. My mind was trying really hard to take one step at a time, but my body was not reacting. I believe there is a very powerful disconnect between your senses, your body, and your mind. I am not sure if it is protective or destructive.

Chapter 1— First Steps

The Compass

The compass guides us where we need to go,
the compass saves us from getting lost,
the compass brings us back to where we started.

All directions lead to you;
with the compass's help, the journey is easy.
It does not matter which direction you go,
you will always be able to find your way.

Without the compass
I will get lost,
my life will become foggy,
my meaning will disappear.

You are my compass.
You right me when I am wrong,
you lead me where I need to go,
you save me from myself.

No matter what direction I go,
whether it is east, west, north, or south,
I know that you will be with me
and forever be my compass.

One day, about nine months after Barb left us, I looked at Jack, our dog, and said aloud, "This is ridiculous." Right then, I knew if I did not make a choice to walk farther and faster, I was literally going to die. I believe, when we lose someone close, we all get to the point of making the choice to live or die.

That walk changed my life. While I was on that first long walk, my first poem came streaming in and would not get out of my head until I wrote it down. Unfortunately, I did not have a pen and paper and had to keep saying it over and over for two miles until I made it to a downtown Starbucks and could borrow a pen and take a napkin. I was greatly relieved to put the following words to paper.

Chapter 1 — First Steps

I Found GOD Within

I found GOD in the wind
I found GOD in the sun
I found GOD in the water
I found GOD in the sky

I found GOD within

I found GOD in death
I found GOD in life
I found GOD in tears
I found GOD in laughter

I found GOD within

I found GOD in a dog's eye
I found GOD in a cat's call
I found GOD in a flower
I found GOD in silence

I found GOD within

I found GOD in the ocean
I found GOD in the mountains
I found GOD in the streams
I found GOD in the deserts

I found GOD within

I found GOD in a book
I found GOD in music
I found GOD in meditation
I found GOD in the light

I found GOD within

I found GOD in fear
I found GOD in love
I found GOD in pain
I found GOD in work

I found GOD within

Chapter 1 — First Steps

Walking farther and faster each day allowed me to talk to Barb. I got angry. I told her I loved her and demanded more, sometimes in the same sentence. I think when we are in the middle of grief, we humans think we can control everything by doing what we always do. What we do not realize is that grieving is one of those times when we can no longer have any control over what matters the most. The fog I was in did not seem quite as dense, allowing me to get glimpses of reality outside of myself.

Finding Love

Why is it when you cannot find love,
it is staring you in the face.

Why is it when you need an answer,
you do not hear it being whispered to you.

Why is it that when fear takes hold,
love is hiding in the mist.

Why is it when pain takes over,
it is allowed a voice.

Why is it when you see a miracle,
it cannot be seen for what it is.

LIFE

Chapter 1—First Steps

Each of my walks took on a life of its own. Usually, in addition to what was going on in my mind, I was experiencing some sort of physical pain in my back or my leg. These long-distance walks were a battle between my stubbornness and my aging body. Typically, what would happen is I would target a bench at the halfway mark so I could sit and recuperate. If that doesn't make you feel old, nothing will. I understood reaching the bench was an accomplishment. It not only gave me a goal, but it also allowed me to find a venue to play in my thoughts.

Two Souls

*Two souls
one connection.
One on earth, one in spirit,
joined together by a common cause,
to help mankind heal.*

*Death is not the end,
it is only the beginning.
Working together to produce the results,
that will help you and me cope.*

*Never selfish, always true.
The two together give the concert of the heavens,
that each of us will understand.*

*So mourn if you must,
grieve until it hurts.
But know that the connection is greater now.*

Chapter 1—Frist Steps

People have moments in their lives when they are going along minding their own business and a song comes through, hitting home. You have probably heard it before but not truly listened. All of a sudden, this song opens a door, and the words speak directly to you. I call these theme songs. I think, when you lose someone, you grab on to these theme songs because they not only touch your heart but move you to a safer place.

One song that did this for me was Tyrone Wells' song, "More." He speaks volumes to me with a few lines:

> I think we are all afraid that we might be alone down here. We all want to have some faith. At least that's true in my case to just believe. I've seen the heights reminding me I'm alive. I don't want to die.
>
> I don't want to waste another day or night. I know there is something more than what we are living for.

Feeling safe after losing someone in your life is an extraordinary and profound experience. Allowing yourself this gift of falling into the theme song will at least give you one moment of calmness and hopefully the realization that healing is possible.

Theme Song

Sometimes when you hear a song
it can take you away
to places unknown.

A theme song of your life
can relinquish control,
to allow you to dream
of a place that could be real,
or a feeling of security.

Be in the moment
with your current thoughts,
but allow the theme song
to restore your balance for the future.

Theme songs
are not used to escape
the realities of your life.
They smooth the hills of emotions,
to land you softly among yourself.

Chapter 1 — First Steps

I want to return to what walking means to me. If I were going to give any advice to anyone after the loss of a loved one, it would be to walk. Take the first step whether you feel like it or not. Here is what I see happening if you do not. Imagine a tree being planted. It takes root slowly and grows. Things happen around it, but it never goes anywhere. Pretty soon, it loses its leaves, and although it may come back, it may also wither from a lack of attention. Do not be a tree. Take the step that could save your spirit.

Walking Backwards

Walking backwards in your footsteps,
seeing the depression of the soul,
finding help within its canyons,
requires very little but letting go.

Following the steps backwards in time,
takes you to places you have already been.
Who or what came by before you,
is found only in your imagination.

Finding hope in the footsteps committed
is the art of letting go,
and opening your heart
to have the feelings that you did not think you had anymore.

Walking backwards in your footsteps,
allows me to go with you on your journey,
if only for a momentary flight of fantasy.

Chapter 2

Men Don't Cry

*The lights of life create a clear pathway for all to unite
in the sparkles of joyful remembrance of Love's embrace.
~ Archangel Raphael*

Guys are not supposed to cry—at least that is what I thought, and what a lot of other men who grew up in the fifties think. Macho feelings are held close to the vest, and if you are going to cry, do it in the privacy of your own home. Here is my opinion on that. *Baloney!* If you don't lose the "manhood" trap, keeping your feelings bottled up is just darned destructive and a waste. Allowing yourself the honor of grieving and releasing the emotions puts you in control of moving forward.

Stop-Sign Tears

Pulling up slowly,
lost in thoughts of the past,
never knowing when it will hit you.
Tears glide down with surprise.

Thoughts that you are beyond it
flash out and bring you back into the dream.
What is different with this moment, and why now?

Realizing that you cannot control
the feelings hidden in the creases of your identity,
allow yourself the freedom to be who you need to be.

Go within and know that it is good to remember.
Never forget, never regret.
Growth as a human allows you to take the feelings with you.

Also, you might want to step on the gas,
and leave the stop sign behind you.
It will be there for another day.

Chapter 2 — Men Don't Cry

At times during this trip you are on, you need to stop. Take stock of the direction you are going. See if everyone is in the vehicle. You do not want to leave someone at the gas station, but if you do, it would be a good thing to turn around and retrieve him or her.

Okay, you are probably thinking: *What the heck does this little story have to do with anything?* What I have found on this journey is that I've spent so much time trying to save myself that I may not have been doing a good enough job keeping everyone in the car. When you lose someone, a really good lesson is to learn to keep checking to see if everyone is moving in the same direction and whether help might be needed. The ultimate goal should be for all the people involved to reach the destination at the same time, without too much damage.

Lesson learned.

Second Guesses

Second guesses are like putty.
Slippery and shiny on the outside,
and soft and flowing on the inside.

Second guesses are like rain on a sunny day.
Sparkling with the sun's rays,
but wet and cold, just the same.

Second guesses can be planted.
Watered,
raised to mature
but never really helping to resolve.

Be aware of second guesses.
Acknowledge them,
bow to them,
but treat them as they should be.
Part of the road to recovery.

Chapter 2 — Men Don't Cry

I definitely cannot speak for everyone else who has lost a spouse or other loved one, but for me, holidays during that first year was extraordinarily challenging. Barb treasured Thanksgiving and Christmas the most. In November, I realized I had done nothing. I had not collected gifts for the past two months and hidden them in the closet. I had not gone to the Dollar Store and bought out the candy section. I had not put any thought into what to get special friends and family members. For the previous twenty-five years, I had personally decorated the outside of the house with lights and moving animals. That year, it had not crossed my mind at all.

When I started thinking about it, my question was, "What the heck is going on?" I believe in my heart I was doing my own version of a peaceful protest. Yeah, I know—flashback. Without getting too analytical about myself, I think that was one of the few ways I could still protest what had happened. A really close friend reminded me that traditions are not just mine; they're shared experiences. And I remember thinking she was right. For the first time, I heard something that made sense and seemed to register somewhere deep down, which helped motivate me to get out of the state I was in.

The lesson here for those of us on this ship is to not forget the important things we have done in the past. Get involved. Get input. Make changes if you want to, but do not let your protest change what is important to remember. It may hurt, but instead of protesting, think of the traditions in your life as a gift.

Quiet Peace

*Floating through time,
waiting for something to happen.
The longer you get away,
death stops taking such a firm grip.*

*Reflecting about how you feel now,
seems so hard to place into perspective.
But so much has occurred
since your former reality.*

*Your only reliance
is to take stock about how you feel,
and let love guide you
to a place that was so hard to get too.*

*What does it feel like
where you are?
I have come to a place that everyone seeks.
The place of quiet peace.*

My family and I have been going to Manzanita, Oregon, for a long time. For that first Thanksgiving without Barbara, going to the place that meant so much to us seemed appropriate. I was in complete control of my emotions, blocking out the fact this was the first Thanksgiving without Barb. I had my armor on and was well protected until one of my sons asked, "How are you doing, Dad?"

It is amazing, how fast cracks can appear in your armor. As soon as you think you are in control, life lets you know you are not. Let us just say the rest of the day was spent trying to gray tape the armor together. You have got to love grey tape. Mercifully, the day ended with a hope that the next day would be brighter. It was.

Chapter 2—Men Don't Cry

Where Are You?

*What is the answer to my question, "Where are you?"
You are in the gentle breeze brushing my cheek.
You are in the flock of birds playing in the air.
You are in the seed floating past.
You are in my mind playing with me.*

*You begin to arrive the day you died,
to remind me that life has meaning and we are never apart.
I have been waiting to continue the conversation,
now realizing that we have been doing it all along.*

*So I am going to stop asking, "Where are you?"
Instead, I am going to feel you in everything I do.
Gentle peace,
Quiet contemplation,
anger and devotion.*

*It does not matter.
Because I know you are here.
Forever connected,
realizing the fear.*

*That you are forever reminding me that your presence begins,
and ends with the thought that I do not have to ask,
"Where are you?"*

Chapter 3

Tackling Yourself

*Each step connects dots that you set forth long ago.
Movement in light is your eternal compass
of Love's holy gifts.
~ Archangel Raphael*

I just returned from a vacation to the Virgin Islands. My eldest son and daughter-in-law thought that because I had not had a vacation in a long time, I needed to get away from the unseen risks associated with the death of a spouse. So, I flew across the country. I took three planes, two taxis, and a ferry to get to the hope of my salvation. Once I got over the travel shock, I looked around and realized where I was. It suddenly occurred to me you can travel around the world and still be in the same mental frame of mind no matter where you go.

So on day three I swam with the fish and found something I had lost—me. Swimming with millions of juvenile fish was magical. There were so many fish, it seemed like I could walk on their backs to the beach. It was a life-altering experience. My suggestion for anyone who has lost a spouse is to look at yourself when you are ready and find your passion. This in turn will help in finding the real you.

We all know how important that is in moving on. Swim with the fish. Adopt a dog. Volunteer in your community. Find yourself and your passion. I will be there to cheer you on.

Tackling Ghosts

Those that go home before us,
take with them small pieces
of each of us left behind.

Looking over a lifetime so far,
we are surrounded by memories
of fathers, mothers, sisters and brothers,
sons and daughters, grandmothers and grandfathers.

You choose how you treat the ghosts of the past.
Freedom comes when you can remember
each and every one of them
as contributing to your current path.

Good or bad, happy or sad,
tackle the ghosts with grace.
Keep your heart open to the lessons learned,
and rejoice that they are still with you.

Discovering yourself can be shocking at times. You think you are strong and that you are becoming an independent person for the first time in more than thirty years. Relying on others in your life suddenly helps you realize you continue in the same state of being you have always been in.

I think being aware you want to move forward in your humanness is a good step in understanding that the process is harder than you think. It takes time and effort to take control of the forces that keep you from moving in the direction you want to go. I understand now it is a balancing act between independence and reliance. Both are good, but controlling the mixture makes a better recipe.

Chapter 3—Tackling Yourself

Slow Treadmill

I feel like I am on a slow treadmill and running fast.
My heart knows there is an answer.
My mind wants it now.

For every question there is an answer.
But I cannot hear it,
because I am running too fast.

Life's mysteries are at my fingertips.
Communication is just a heartbeat away,
but my pace needs to slow to the right speed.

Linking the energy by request,
coming into alignment with the vibration on both sides,
requires little but intention.

Now that the answer is known,
slow down,
take a breath,
require nothing,
and the connection will occur because it can.

Being on an emotional roller coaster really sucks. As a man, I am reminded, somewhere in the back of my mind, that we should not show emotion. I identify with people who have bipolar tendencies. You can be so happy one second; then the next, a bolt of lightning can hit you and you find yourself a wiggling bowl of Jell-O. A picture, a song, a smell, or a voice can lead to these wild ups and downs. I'm not saying it isn't normal, but it is darned exhausting. You're hoping it will end someday, but at the same time, it's what keeps you connected. So you keep moving forward, not knowing what's around the corner to provoke or be a joy. Hmm…sounds like life.

Chapter 3 — Tackling Yourself

A Need to Be Sad

A need to be sad looms,
like ground-hugging fog
covering everything in its path.

Sun breaks through,
shining into the face.
Music of the angels
plays in the mind.

Time does not change anything,
it only puts space into the sadness.
Waiting for the wave to break over the rock
brings momentary relief.

Take the sadness with you.
Use it wisely,
and go into the future,
knowing you can.
Grow to meet yourself.

Chapter 4

The New Normality

*Opening the curtains to share light in the daily dance of life,
honors the eternal connection of Love's extension with all.*
~ Archangel Raphael

During the first year without Barbara, I got into the habit of talking to myself. I probably always had, but now I noticed. I think I was trying to determine whether I would have a good answer to one of my many questions about life and death. After all, if I talked to myself, I did not have to subject anyone else to these uncomfortable questions. With that in mind, I was asking myself, *What is "normal"?* According to the dictionary, it means "regular, usual, or natural." I think my "normal" shifted away from what I thought was my center.

When you are with someone for so long, "normal" becomes second nature—a daily existence that is always there. You can count on it and set your clock by it. But I noticed that after losing someone, "normal" no longer looks the same. It noticeably shifts, reflecting a new version of normal. And in a way, it takes you away from your previous comfort zone. Survival depends on your being able to perceive this shift, to adjust to the new normality, and to grasp its significance.

Moving into and accepting this new normality allowed me to desire this new life in spite of grasping my old center with one hand. Even now, I assume eventually I will let go of that old center when the time feels right.

Freedom

Slowly gliding over the mud flats,
where white shells litter the bottom.
Flat fish dart in all directions,
seeking peace from the world.

Flowing with the current,
feeling you are hardly moving.
Birds fish in the shallows,
sea lions poke their heads above the waves.
Letting go of all sounds of mankind.

Catching the fast-moving water,
while moving quickly in the canoe,
requires little effort,
freeing yourself to feel the sun.

Finding peace.
Letting go.
Freedom.
Seek them in everything you do.
Look at what is in front of you and pay attention.

During the process of coming through the darkness of the first six months after Barbara's death, I did not cook at all. My kids and I were in survival mode and lived strictly on frozen meals. Not only did I have a very limited cooking vocabulary, but I also had no interest in it—none. Walking into the kitchen one day, I saw everyone standing in front of the open refrigerator, staring and grumbling something about fresh foods. I knew then I needed to step up to the reality plate and figure something out. From that point, my promise was to cook twice a week after I found out some genius had invented something called a Crock-Pot. It's this thing you can put a whole lot of ingredients into in the morning and magically have a dinner at the end of the day.

To me, cooking has been a life lesson. Take a bunch of ingredients that include friendship, good advice, and love from family and friends. Put them into an empty vessel. Turn on the life lights, stir the contents, and watch what happens. What you get is something new that does not necessarily look like what was put into the pot, but hopefully this outcome is something improved.

I love the Crock-Pot. I would like to thank whoever invented such an amazing thing for making me not only a great cook but a better version of myself.

Chapter 4 — The New Normality

The Leaf

The leaf hangs on,
with winter in full stride,
fluttering in the breeze,
daring anyone to knock it off.

It strives to keep being,
to be the last one standing,
in its communication with God.

It does not realize,
that just letting go,
brings it closer
than it has ever been,
to the source it seeks.

Lessons are learned,
but oftentimes its faith
is not strong enough,
and so it holds on.

Sometimes you need to step away from yourself and look at the bigger picture. What happened in Haiti during and after the earthquake put life and death onto a whole different playing field for me. No words can describe the emotions the folks of Haiti experienced. In my own little bubble with my own little problems, I looked at what was on television and could only imagine what losing my family, let alone every child, was like. My heart went out to the Haitians for the great loss they suffered. I knew it would take a very long time for them to recover both physically and spiritually. My hope was that each and every one of them would have the love and support I'd had in response to my loss. But short of that, I hope they at least got the help they needed.

Life and Death

*Seen by itself,
the randomness of life and death,
creates a complicated message to the masses.*

*Seen within the bigger picture
of time and space,
and spirit and grace,
it brings different conclusions.*

*Missing someone is all and good,
but seeing them in a better place
brings importance to the existence
of the human race.*

*It ties the circle
of why we are all here.
Putting things into perspective
with a sense of completion.*

Hope is like the ripples caused by a pebble dropped into a pond. They start at the center and spread out until they can go no farther. They want to move out and gather speed, creating a self-sustaining energy. Hope does not always work out the way you want, but without it, your light can go out. A lot happened during the year of Barb's death: new jobs, new friends, and new experiences took place. I had hope for the future and all that it could bring. Compared to when I first started writing, my existing state is a miracle in itself.

Hope spreads like wildfire and can be contagious. Henry Ford's words come to mind: "If you think you can or you think you can't, you're right." My suggestion is to think you can and to spread hope to everyone you know. No matter what transpires in your life, never give up hope. Without hope you will never know what could have been.

Chapter 4 — The New Normality

Hope

*Hope continues to exert its influence,
bringing comfort to the lost,
and peace to the mind.*

*It allows you to travel farther
than you thought
you could go.*

*Holding onto it
does not always give you the answer,
but it sees you through the tough times
and requires nothing in return.*

I thought I was going to be a train wreck during the anniversary week of Barb's death. I fully expected to be sucked back into the fog, as I call it. Although I remember in great detail the whole last week of her life, I was a little surprised that the anniversary of her death turned out to be just another day for me. Of course, I thought a lot about that day a year ago, but I did not react the way I thought society expected me too. In analyzing myself, what I believe I discovered was this. My son told me I had become very transparent since Barb's death, which I think was a compliment. I took *transparency* to mean that I am open and honest and, as we used to say, I tell it like it is.

I communicate with Barb every day. I discuss the highs and the lows and the happy and the sad. I ask for guidance, direction, and peace. I think allowing myself that daily venting has helped make "time" less important. After all, if you listen to some folks, we humans have made up the whole time thing anyway. My theory is that because I have ongoing communication, when the dreaded one-year anniversary came around, subconsciously I knew it was just another day. Time was my problem, not hers. I guess what I learned is that time is a structure we do not have to subscribe to. Allowing yourself the honor and pleasure of communicating as you see fit breaks down the walls that restrict you and allows you the freedom to not be caught up in the time dilemma.

Leaving

How am I supposed to feel?
You left me a year ago.
It seems so sudden,
so selfish,
so permanent.

Is it like the mother bird
that pushes the baby
out of the nest and says "Fly"?

Is it the knowing that you are surrounded
by the ones who have left before you,
and you will not have the answer to "Why?"

How to proceed.
How to cope.
How to respond.
How to try.

Unanswered questions
create the feelings
that bring you into reality,
and get you by.

Chapter 5

That Dreaded Question

Your holy purpose is to extend Love's embrace.
Remember your light opens your dance
to unite with others in a new tempo.
~ Archangel Raphael

It's two o'clock in the morning, and I'm finding myself wide-awake after a day of, let me say, interesting twists and turns. I stopped by a friend's office earlier today. We used to work together and it had been over a year since I had seen her. The question out of her mouth, "So, how is Barb?" sent me into a place I did not want to go.

It was such a simple question, and my brain tried to come up with something cute to say. I think she sensed something was coming when nothing came out of my mouth. After what seemed an eternity, I finally told her Barb had died. I do not know if I did that for the shock value or because I felt by now, everyone in the whole world should have already known. After all, the world had stopped spinning on its axis when she died.

I apologized for not having any other way to inform her, and from that moment on, for the rest of the day, I felt numb. I thought I had been singled out to withstand the onslaught of loss. But I had made it. A year had passed, and I could put my emotions to bed. Well, maybe not. A four-word sentence proved to me that although I'd really and truly thought I'd come a long way, which I am sure I had in some respects, I had just been treading water. Beneath the surface are a whole lot of potential landmines that can take you back to times and places you might prefer to keep locked up. I think it is human that these events do occur. It makes the journey real and unpredictable.

That night, I sat in silence, with only the refrigerator moaning in the background. I had hope that the next time I encounter the last person on earth who does not know Barb has died, I will be able to answer that question in a more humane way. And, just maybe, I will not have to be sitting up late at night thinking what a weird day it was.

Direct Connect

I wish I could send you an e-mail.
Tell you how things are going,
see your reply,
argue over what I am not doing with the kids.

I wish I could call you.
Have you tell me about your day,
working with the angels,
and learning so much.

I wish I could write you a letter.
Send it to heaven COD,
wait for your response,
with a return address out of this world.

How do you know you have found love? Was it lost? Did it pass you on the street and you did not see it? For those of us who have lost love, how do you know when the time is right to allow yourself to find it again? How many people have told you it is required that you wait a year, two years, or even five years? I'm lead to wonder how do you know you have found love:

Why is this?

Do you become less human after you have lost someone?

Does the capacity to give of yourself get any less real?

Is the loneliness we feel so unimportant that we cannot possibly be rational in our thinking?

Although you think you are giving wise and sane advice and it is coming from your heart, *stop it*. Step back, think about what you are telling those who have lost their love, and think about why you are saying it. I think you will realize, although you have good intentions, I—and all of us who have lost a loved one—deserve to be happy and loved. Let us be in control of finding, losing, and deciding the timing. Feeling guilty for loving someone new would be the last thing I would ever place on anyone else's shoulders.

Chapter 5 — The Dreaded Question

The Veil

*The veil lifted this morning.
Everything became bright and clear.
No matter what happens going forward,
choice controls the outcome.*

*Destiny lingers on the horizon,
and up till now it could not be grasped.
But, clearly, the lens of uncertainty
brings the life back into focus.*

*We are all on our own time schedules,
facing the darkness,
achieving the victories.
But, when the veil is lifted,
smiling with purpose takes on a whole new meaning.*

Did you ever do those connect-the-dots pictures as a kid? I used to love following the numbers and seeing what was going to show up on the page in the end. My life is like that. I move ahead and away from the death of my wife by connecting the dots. Let me give you an example. I met a really wonderful couple one weekend. They came to me because his mother had read an article about my journey in the Oregonian newspaper. This couple had written a book, *Send Me a Sign*, a story about their journey after the death of the husband's first wife. You could say this was all coincidence and just write it off as an interesting thing that happened. I saw it as an example of one thing leading to another, leading to another.

Since Barb's death, I have felt guided when following the dots. What I do is step back, watch what comes up, and accept with amazement the dots that appear. I accept the people I meet along the way with open arms and mind, not necessarily knowing at the time what the reason is for meeting them. I have faith I am being guided down the right path and the dots of my life are going to eventually create a picture that will make perfect sense. Sometimes I become impatient waiting for the next dot to appear and have to tell myself everything is as it is supposed to be—in other words, to take a "chill pill" and to go with the flow. Boy, I have not said those words in a long time.

I think all of us who have lost someone to death need to be able to hold on to something that will get us to the next stage in our lives. Connecting the dots is my solution to this dilemma, and I would highly recommend everyone look out for his or her own dots to connect and then follow that path until the picture is complete. It may surprise you.

The Path

Connect the dots
along your path,
seeing people
for the first time or last.

Watch the signs,
and reflect on the connection,
that bring the daily miracles
into your worldly focus.

Choose to react,
or merely watch it happen.
Being open to the possibilities,
will send light to your soul.

Chapter 6

The Silence

*Love conquers all. Inspired Love weaves eternity into daily prayers
that are folded into life's passion of knowing another day.
~ Archangel Raphael*

Every once in a while the world stops, and I find myself sitting at my desk surrounded by work, being unable to move and totally lost in thought, so to speak. I know music is playing in the background, but I don't really hear it. I know the birds continue to fly around outside my window, but I don't really see them. I am stuck in no man's land, and emotional bombs from the past are exploding in my mind. I am lost on the battlefield, not knowing what is going on around me.

Where do you go in moments like this? Eventually, I come back and realize what I am doing and where I am. The sounds and the feelings return. My point is, even though we think we are okay and are moving ahead, moments of what I call *The Silence* envelope us. Anyone watching me would probably think I was in some great meditation session. I do not fear this and quite honestly appreciate the peace that comes over me, if only for a few minutes. I think this is the spirit's way of allowing you a timeout to quiet the mind and continue the healing.

    Take advantage of it.

Chapter 6 — The Silence

What Now?

When you are questioning
the direction of your life's choices,
what now?

When you cannot see through
the mist of uncertainty,
what now?

When you come to the fork in the road,
and you are confused
about the right way to go,
what now?

Having the answers
ahead of time,
would only allow you
a temporary reprieve.

Any choice,
any direction,
is the right one for the moment.
It will lead you to the same place.

One day, I sat looking at my clothes closet and realized all the ways my life had changed since Barb's death. When Barb was alive, we each had half the closet. Most of the time we were fairly satisfied with sharing the closet, and I admit my half often crossed into hers. I do not think either one of us was really into clothes, especially Barb. She never was good at buying things for herself. She put most of her efforts into providing for the kids and me.

That day, this was my dilemma: Looking at that same space, I realized I had completely taken over the closet with my material world. I did not understand how that was possible. It wasn't like I was going out and buying stuff all the time. I hate shopping. So, either the amount of my stuff was growing or something else was going on. I have to believe this is a metaphor for my life in moving away from Barb's death through recovery and coming into my own identity. This space had been "us," and now it is "me."

Honestly, I don't think I liked it very much. I knew the goal was to move on, but I thought my solution should be to go clean out my closet. I hoped it also meant that by starting to notice the little changes in our lives we hadn't before, it is a sign we are ready: ready to notice, ready to receive, ready to interpret, and, unfortunately or not, ready to move in a new direction that will require a huge amount of bravery.

Softly

Singing softly
under my breath,
means peace
has entered my soul.

Crying loudly
comes no more,
to share the spaces of grief.

Realizing things have changed,
is a major event
not to be taken lightly.

Only when you notice
the subtle changes,
can you go to the next level
within the safety of your own mind.

Chapter 6—The Silence

What does success in coping with death mean to you? Does it mean you can now walk your dog through the neighborhood and actually look up and smile as people go by? Does it mean you went and bought flowers for the oak barrel that has been neglected for the past year? Does it mean you made chocolate chip cookies for the first time in God knows how long? Or did you just go for a ride without crying or talk to your kids about something stupid and inconsequential?

As you have probably guessed, there are no secret answers to this process. There are feelings, emotions, perceptions, and the heartfelt daily views of others going through their own loss. I have found others share the need to know what it is like on a daily basis, *not* what the pundits of grief say we should be experiencing. I have found it helpful to talk and write about this day-to-day reality.

So back to my initial question, "What does success in coping with death mean to me?" Yes to all the above, but remember it is something different for everyone. There is no right or wrong. To me, being human means I do not have to be like the people around me and react in the same way they do. Neither do you. So create your own successes, notice life, and react with your own style. If you are not there yet, you will be, and I wish you the best on your own very special journey.

Long and Short

The longest, shortest year of my life,
brings peace when needed,
sadness when required,
loneliness around the edges.

It fights to conquer fear,
celebrates the many victories,
and darkens the doorstep
with surprising timing.

Reaching out and knowing
that the further you get away
from the longest, shortest year,
will bring peace at last
to the place you got away from.

March 14, 2010, would have been our thirty-fifth wedding anniversary, and I forgot it. How is that even possible? On the morning of the fifteenth, it dawned on me that I'd forgotten it for the first time—well, unless, I counted the time I forgot the anniversary card at home while we were on vacation. Awkward; but wait, what does it mean? Was this some pseudo-analysis mumbo-jumbo explanation? Like, deep down after making it through this past year I somehow intentionally blanked it out? That'll teach you, Barb! I guessed she was a little too busy where she was to put much thought into a particular day. Could it be I really did not place any relevance on the date any longer and had made it just another day?

After spending so long with someone, I knew that wasn't the answer. No, I had to rationalize that for me, the days had just blended together. And even though the holidays and anniversaries the year before were so extremely hard, I was being protected from the extremes of emotions that hurt. I decided to think of it as Barb's gift to me, for without that, I was just another selfish man who'd forgotten an anniversary. And I just couldn't let that be.

Chapter 6 — The Silence

A Day in Time

A day in time,
suddenly forgotten,
means only that it is a day in time.

Seeking meaning
to what is left behind,
puts you at the crossroads
of your truest purpose.

Without time to confuse and contort,
you are free to choose what is ahead
without remorse.

Never regret
what you cannot control.
Time only puts limits
within the boundaries of your thinking.

Everything is perfect.
Everything has a reason.
Seeing the truth without the constraints,
is the freedom we all seek.

Sometimes I think a person caught in the numbness of grief does not necessarily think through what he or she is doing. It is almost like being in a naïve state of mind. I found myself wondering about what I would say to God if I were to write him or her a letter:

Dear God,

Thank you for coming to listen. I hope this does not sound too petty. Sitting on the beach at sunset, watching the opaque green waves, I reflect on my relationship with you.

I sometimes wonder whether what I thought was a relationship was just you, putting up with the ego of a flawed human being. I always believed and, even as a kid, knew you were there. Through the ups and downs of my life, were you there with me? Or was it just blind luck that I made it this far? I remember so many times being physically saved and thinking it was you. But, of course, I went back to what I was doing which most of the time was raising a family.

Chapter 6 — The Silence

Over the past year there have been many times when I have been listening and have been amazed at the events going on around me. Spiritually, I have grown so much and look forward to whatever outcome and path you would like to help me with.

Not unlike all people before me, I wonder what the purpose is. Have I set this all up myself, or am I carrying out some huge planned life map? Do you really have an opinion on how it really turns out? Why do I have a sense you're involved in everything I do, but a detachment that tells me it all ends up in the same place anyway; is that it?

There are so many paths we cannot see and we get to choose, but the result is all the same. If that is the case, I would like to thank you for being along on the trip. Thank you for taking care of our loved ones who have already ventured your way, and have that beach chair ready for me when the time is right. I would like to listen to the waves with you.

To Remember

Sentimentally speaking,
looking at the past does not shed light
on the future.

What it does do is give peace within
the framework of safety.

Knowing that the journey begins now,
no matter what transpired in the past,
brings comfort to the spirit and helps
in shedding the ego-controlled world.

Move forward in peace,
knowing that the hug from Heaven
guides you on your journey to take
you back to the start of remembrance.

Chapter 7

Unexpected Strength

*Love nourishes the patterns within your life,
bringing wholeness to your soul.
Acknowledge your "now" in awareness that Love never ends.
~ Archangel Raphael*

One day, it occurred to me to reflect on what I have learned in the first year since Barb's death. That sentence is easy to write, but another thing to actually answer. Surely I have learned things that will affect the rest of my life here on this planet. Caught up in grief that was all-consuming for at least half that time taught me that men can get angry enough to think they are rational when demanding that communication continue. And not only communication, but also when expecting what I call the daily miracles. They are required and have been a natural part of my daily life of moving forward.

Come on now, don't normal people move on after someone dies and not require proof that the one they lost is listening? Heck, I don't know. I'm just asking the question. If I thought I was normal, I probably would not be writing this in the first place. I have learned I can walk farther than I thought, ride a bike and look cool at the same time, and hike into the woods while listening for that voice that I can hear only when the wind is blowing through the trees. I have learned a family can survive the loss and get stronger day by day. I have learned kids are resilient and make it their quest to remind you that in some ways you now have become the child. Also, you are not allowed to die for a very long time. That would be unacceptable. I have learned how lonely life is without that long-term relationship. I have learned I can love again, given the opportunity.

I have learned I can cook and I can be overwhelmed by the monthly bills, just like Barb did. I have also learned life does not stop because someone dies. Real emotions are lessons that have changed me, and I expect that I will never again be satisfied with things that are not important at a deep level. I have learned I have to work really hard to care about my career except from the standpoint of where I am going; and how important is it, really? I have learned I have friends and others who love me, even when I do not have the strength to give it back.

Wow, I guess I really did learn some lessons. But are they the right ones? I sense I will find that out someday. May your lessons be special and be guided by love like mine have been. I will continue to learn and apply these lessons so I can hope to maintain a direction that means something to me and to those around me.

Hope arises in all of us, and death is not the end. No matter what you believe, your own lessons can strengthen you and help guide you after the death of someone who is important in your life.

Silence

*Falling into silence,
reflecting on what was lost,
only threatens the security
of the individual.*

*Life continues onward,
as people go about their business.
The awareness of the world,
never noticing the dimness of the individual.*

*Eventually pieces of different puzzles
transform the new individual
to a different kind of world,
forever changing the past.*

*It is not bad.
It is not good.
It is not complete.
It is not understood.*

*It just is.
It is just choices.
Without choices,
there is no moving forward.*

Chapter 7 — Unexpected Strength

If a tree falls in the forest and no one is there to hear it, does it make a sound? How about this one: If a man slices the top of his finger while no one is around, what do you hear? In my case, let us just say if anyone had been around, he or she would have heard some really creative words and then seen some manly bandage making.

Cutting my finger did make me think, though. While Barb was alive and the kids were younger, I could count on someone's being around if I did something stupid. In fact, I remember being on an extension ladder, hanging on for dear life and trying to cut a piece of aluminum at the roofline. Of course, I was doing this in front of a picture window while the whole family watched. Might as well make it interesting, huh? Well, you can guess what was going to happen. Yep, fingers slice faster than metal. Flying off the ladder without touching the rungs from that height is kind of tricky. I was looking over at the window and seeing the family looking at me.

That's family for you. But when I did basically the same thing again, no one was there. It made me think about the changes that have occurred. Oh, it's still the same stupidity, but I can only share it with myself now. That's what hit home. If you have family around, enjoy the day-to-day events because you never know about tomorrow. When that still small voice in your head says to be careful, step away from the tools and go do something safe.

Some Days

Some days move like snails,
as a slow progression to an unknown outcome.

Some days speed like the comet,
going so fast but not taking anything in.

Some days require a Herculean effort,
to place one foot in front of the other.

Some days are so exciting that you cannot wait
to get to the ending so you can see if it matched your wishes.

But whether it is a snail's pace, comet's tail,
a trial, a movement, or the mastered ending,
you create the picture of what you want to see,
and set in motion the outcome of your destiny.

If you could carry on a conversation with God, what would you say or ask? I was sitting at a lacrosse game and watching the sun play hide-and-seek among the clouds, when the thought of God's calling me on my cell phone crossed my mind. Before you ask, no; I do not sit around all day and think of these things. They just pop in unannounced, seeing if I am going to react to them. The visual alone of God calling on my cell phone was priceless. Okay, so I'll play along.

"This is Mike. How can I help you?" I have answered the phone like that for twenty-five years, so habits are hard to break.

"Oh, hi, God. I'd like to sit and talk for a while, if that is okay with you?"

I think I would want to know how her or his day went and if anything special happened: "What is the weather like where you are? Is there weather? Or are you everywhere at the same time so you have it all?

"What is your favorite color and why? Oh, and what about how humans treat each other on this planet? Is there right or wrong and does it really matter in the end? Do you really judge us, or are we just on our own?"

This is probably where I would sneak in the question of why my wife had to die. I am kind of hoping the other questions would be distracting and that last one would be easy to answer. I would want to know if I am doing the right things for my family and if I am really going to make it.

I would want to know if he or she likes the bathroom tile I put in and whether he thinks I will ever finish that project. I would ask why we just cannot see our loved ones who are on the other side so that we can know everything is great with them. Is it really necessary that humans mourn so much? As a longtime manager, I always look for the efficient short cut. Pain just seems so darn consuming, in all aspect of your life, not just time.

I would want to know whether we are going to destroy ourselves, or if, as I believe, there is always hope. I would want to know how she or he feels about things and whether guidance is there if we are just willing to open ourselves up to it: "What advice can you give me personally that will allow me to believe that you are listening?"

I know this is all about faith and I really do not expect answers. It does make me think, though. What questions would you ask? Go ahead and ask your questions. Treat it like a cathartic moment.

For once, you are in control. Oh, and by the way, I am thinking you might want to answer the phone next time it rings. You never know who is going to be on the other end.

Catharsis

I need a cathartic moment.
A miracle unseen,
saving me from myself,
to prove what I already have.

I need to know the path
is really in front of me,
that our venture is real,
while looking for the spark
to light my way.

If you have given me everything I have asked for,
then why does my ego make me think it is not enough?

A cathartic moment is only as good
as that moment in time,
never really satisfying the need to know it all.

I need to be accepting
that you will give me what is required,
and stop questioning the forever nature of my ego's grief.

How are you supposed to feel? With more time that goes by, I notice most people expect you to either move on or totally ignore the elephant in the room. Moving on is an option if we are willing to let go of the past and focus on the future. Speaking from experience, I've observed you can move on and not forget. I think what happens is that we put on our "everything is okay" mask and people see we have "moved on."

My guess is this is exactly what they want to see. But really, it should not be about what they want but about whether you feel comfortable within yourself to take the step you need to take. As far as the elephant, it is interesting that even though a lot of people know about death, it is usually easier for them to focus on you. I think it is simply a protective mechanism. I think it is up to us to remember in an appropriate way, whatever that means.

I was driving on Highway 30 to the Oregon coast for business, and I noticed a large number of memorial markers along the road. I could not help but think about all these people who had lost their lives. The markers do not tell their individual stories and are not going to be there forever. At some point, they will disappear, and passersby will not know about those people.

Chapter 7—Unexpected Strength

When I write, I press a button, and it goes out into the ether, continuing on, in theory, forever, like looking at a star that has already exploded in the past, but you are still seeing the light reach your eyes prior to the explosion. This is pretty heavy but fascinating. I know for me, personally, the thought of Barb's traveling through space forever is not only entertaining but also breathtaking.

Talk to the Wind

Talk to the wind,
ride the wave,
see where it goes,
and who it will touch next.

It always answers,
through its gentle pushing and pulling
of nature's gift to mankind.
Feel it against your skin.
Be one with its flow.

Surprise yourself.
Open your heart.
Be with the friend that has always been there,
and never expected anything in return.

Allow the wind to take your thoughts
to other people and places.
Maybe they will listen,
and return the thought someday.

Chapter 8

Different but All the Same

*Light threads through hearts to make a new song.
Each note holds the eternal resonance
of your family's Love song.
~ Archangel Raphael*

During one of my long sanity walks, I suddenly had this image of a painter at the easel with a jar nearby full of variably sized brushes. Right before I saw the image, I was thinking about my family. Connecting the two, I saw each member of the family as a different brush. You know, some are long, some are small, some draw delicate lines, and others are big and sweeping in what they leave behind. You can add the same color to a brush and get a different picture, depending on which brush you use.

One of my sons is a scientist who has to juggle a lot of things but has to be very precise at the same time. Although he might be a bunch of different brushes, underlying everything is a very accurate one that gives sharp definition. One of my daughters is a social worker; she is a typical long brush having to paint the most complete picture quickly and with less detail. She has to size things up fast in her job, as well as in the family, because of assuming the role of oldest female.

My middle son is the film documentarian and probably has to be multiple brushes at the same time. He creates the most dramatic and colorful picture quickly before moving on to the next canvas. A complete picture always comes together in the end, even though the colors seem scattered at times. Another of my sons is the broadest possible brush and is really good at painting the clouds. His brush never completes the picture but the colors are beautiful. The next son paints with one brush only and with determination for his subject. He will paint off the canvas at times but will always return. My younger daughter paints with the tightest-wound brush you can buy and is driven to fill in the lines of her picture while leaving no room for error.

Barb painted with all the brushes available to create a completed family picture. I paint with a wide brush to create the frame for the future. An artist interprets what he or she sees, mixes the colors, and shows respect to his or her subject by putting those brushstrokes on a blank canvas. Even when we have lost someone, the picture was already created and lives forever in the mind of its viewers. Honoring those who are gone with as beautiful a picture as possible made from all those brush strokes is an incredible legacy to their lives.

The Puzzle of Life

*You start out as a thought,
put together with love.*

*You grow into a vessel,
put together with love.*

*Along the way, pieces come and go,
creating a thinker,
put together with love.*

*Even though death is an illusion,
you march towards that end,
never realizing you were put together with love.*

*So, the day comes when the pieces fall apart,
And you really find out,
that you were put together with love.*

Chapter 8 — Different but All the Same

What had the world come to? *Glee* was on the television when I looked outside and saw it pouring. Man, what a lonely world it can be sometimes. I have to laugh at myself occasionally; if I didn't, I would be pretty pitiful. The thought of loneliness creates a picture in my mind that I really do not understand.

Growing up in Arizona, I considered myself to be a loner with a few friends. Somehow I was okay with that. I knew I was self-reliant and everything in my life depended on me. My brother was older, and we really did not have anything in common. I played baseball, swam, and got blown out of the water by the female of the species. I'd worked ever since I could remember; being busy was my way of never being lonely.

When I met my future wife, Barb, I was twenty, and I can honestly say *loneliness* was never in my vocabulary. While raising six kids, loneliness was somehow converted into exhaustion. Then, before I knew it, most of my kids were grown, and my wife was going down the slippery slope of illness. Loneliness started creeping into my life during that time. I do not think you are allowed that feeling, however, because you are too involved in the day-to-day duties taking care of the love of your life.

Then you go through the hardest thing you have ever faced. You start moving away from it over time, and as you do, you realize most of the time your kids have their own lives. Although you know your kids love you, you finally come to the conclusion that their energy, and rightly so, revolves around other things instead of you.

I was not feeling sorry for myself—just growing up, I guess. Maturity is a bummer. With the deepest sincerity, as I sat reflecting on my empty house and all its history, the dog must have been wondering why I was crying.

Does It Matter?

*When your best friend dies,
when the sunset is blue,
when the crow flies by,
does it really matter?*

*When the walk is fast,
and the pain is slow,
when you reach for help,
why should it matter?*

*When you touch someone's face with a smile,
and request to stay connected with your words,
and realize that it only matters to you.*

*Spend a little time on what matters the most,
specialize in the matter of the utmost importance,
the matter of you.*

"Midlife" sounds so stuffy and permanent. You hear a lot about it, but what is it really? To a twenty-year-old, midlife is probably thirty. Think back to when you were twenty. I always thought midlife was halfway to the porch swing that Barb and I were going to share in retirement. Perspective changes quickly.

So now what? Do I have a crisis? What is a crisis, anyway? Is it where you push important people in your life away from you by becoming so complex that the baggage you are carrying to the terminal would weigh down three porters, let alone one? Is it a crisis when you picture yourself on a Harley going cross country after you have sold everything off, just to write a book about people you meet along the way? Is it a crisis when you suddenly shave off the beard that has been attached to your face since the Nixon years?

I think using *crisis* makes it sound like you are in jeopardy of losing your mind instead of taking control of it. Sometimes what may appear to be a rash change to another is just someone's taking back control in his or her life and nothing else. It takes a leap of faith to get to the top of the mountain. A death in your life can profoundly shake up the world as you know it. Also I can tell you that shaving your beard off can get a conversation going with the people around you, especially your younger daughter, who has never seen your chin.

Remember what I said about midlife to a young person? I rest my case.

Purpose

My intended purpose in life
was to grow old gracefully,
with the one I love.

Fate had another plan,
to change that outcome
from destiny to confusion.

Other plans verged,
creating hope that was lost,
and goals that are shared.

A single moment in time
changed the lives forever,
to be bigger and more beautiful
than the original plan ever intended.

Chapter 9

Bravery

*Be you dust or be you stone,
to be what you must just reach out for what you are.
~Yusef (Cat Stevens)*

What is bravery, and how would you define it?

I recently read my friend's journal about the long process of the death of her husband. She wrote about her trials, tribulations, and love of her husband during his illness and, ultimately, his death. Full of poignant memories, her journal brought out all the human traits of caregiving. So much truth is hard to read sometimes, but being a caregiver is such an all-consuming activity. Only a special person can enter that world. What I envisioned by reading this heartfelt journal was a very brave individual who took on a role that no one should have to endure.

Out of love for the dying, we sometimes go beyond what would normally be our comfort level and achieve what can only be considered to be superhuman. I am pretty sure she would not consider herself to be brave. However, when I look at her story from the outside, it, as well as those of many others in the same position, represents ultimate bravery. You take on a role that can be so painful and demeaning that it is like a gunfight in the Old West. Both parties are brave, and most of those watching would not do it. My sister-in-law took on the same role in taking care of my brother during his illness. Until this very moment, I do not think I adequately thanked her for all the care and love she showed him during his death journey.

The rest of us who have not gone through the caregiver story cannot possibly begin to understand that day-to-day existence. We only look on and do not know, or do not want to know, what is really occurring. So, for all the caregivers of the world, you rock, as you are the rocks of your loved ones.

Chapter 9 — Bravery

You Tried To Tell Me

You tried to tell me,
but I would not listen.
Your pain mixed with your dying spirit.

You tried to tell me,
but I would not hear.
You thought we would be better without you.

You tried to tell me,
but I would not see
your body decreasing in energy evidenced in the photos.

Tell me now, I will listen.
Tell me now, I will hear.
Tell me now, I will see.

It is never too late
to say you are sorry.
It is never too late to care.

Those of us who have lost a spouse for any reason know that life usually takes on a whole new meaning. You think about mortality where you might not have before. You become thoughtful of your intentions about your beliefs, your family, your future, and possibly other relationships. After all, the thought of spending the rest of your life alone can scare you to death. So even though you may not be looking for it consciously, a time comes when you suddenly find yourself overwhelmed with emotions that you honestly thought could no longer exist. For whatever reason you use at the time, you fall into the relationship with intention and passion. Nothing else is as important as this connection.

You emerge from the fog of grief with the realization there is life after death in more ways than one. You say things like "You saved my life," and you really mean it. The day comes when your burdens and unrealistic expectations break the bank, so to speak. It can be overwhelming for someone to not only save you, but to take care of you. You allowed your emotions to smother and kill the one thing that brought you out of the fog. Why would anyone knowingly want to take on a project like this? The result is probably not going to be what you were planning. And so it goes, the rest of the story, as Paul Harvey would say.

Chapter 9—Bravery

A good lesson to learn is to separate yourself and your feelings from the emotions of someone paying attention to you. Think about what you really want from a relationship from both sides. And do not put your expectations on the other person without her or his consent. I realize now we have so much love to share but also a shorter time in which to share it.

Remember to look at the whole picture and not just the dream. Becoming someone I was not was never the person I thought I would become. I think it has been long enough that I can step back as if I am viewing myself through someone else's eyes. I look at the person I am now and compare him to the person I thought I was before Barb died. A lot has happened. I have grieved. I have tried to function at work. I have loved and lost. I have discovered I can connect to a power beyond myself and use it to develop new skills. I have become honest, probably to a fault.

Recently, I read a book called *Loving Grief* by Paul Bennett, and one thought hit home. When Barb died, she took my old life with her. Becoming someone new with a focus on the future was now my goal. Could I do it without losing myself completely? I thought so. What I realized is that I needed to come to grips with the idea that I might have to be stronger and say no to things that appear to be too easy. Just because people have done something their whole life does not mean that they need to continue to stay in the same cycle. This is a perfect time for me to step out of the mold and find myself. It's easy to say I have to become someone new, but it's harder to achieve.

First, I had to learn to love myself and to define myself individually without the "couple-ness" that was so easy to hide behind in the past. I had to set the boundaries I was willing to work within, and most importantly, picture what I was supposed to be like when I became the new me. Most people may not see any difference, but I believe what changed was at the spirit level. Reestablishing a foundation on which to build is really important. I know now I was functioning without a base of my own. I believe grief's job is to knock out your foundation so you never feel steady on your feet. When that happens, though, confusion, fright, and loneliness take over.

Then, when someone comes along and shows the willingness to put a couple of nails into the foundation to stabilize it, you are all over it. Grab on, don't let go, and hopefully keep it together. But remember: A couple of nails are temporary fixes, and the walls will come down easily. My personal goal was to build a new foundation from scratch with intelligence, compassion, love, and respect. The result hopefully has been a much stronger me with a capacity to achieve importance in this lifetime.

Chapter 9—Bravery

Live

Live the life you want to,
not the life you think you are supposed to.

Fate has nothing to do with it.
You decide where you fit into the scheme of things.

Hold onto the reality
that you can have the life you want,
but keep in mind you might not need it.

Be thankful for the chance you have,
to live the life you want,
and use it wisely to grow
into what you should have.

Chapter 10

Out of the Cave

*Your beginnings and endings are the same direction,
depending on your viewpoint.
In eternity, Love is the answer to all choices.
~ Archangel Raphael*

The sun hit my face for the first time since, well, I could not remember when. It brought tears to my eyes, not because Barb was gone but because I got to stay here. They were not tears of sadness but tears of joy. I would say that was what is called a breakthrough. Either that, or the sun had killed some of my brain cells. Either way, I was happy. That seems to be the critical statement.

Losing anyone sets you on the path of going through stages that only you can determine. However, the promise that you will get through them and come out of the tunnel into the sunlight is somewhere in the back of your mind. Most people come through in time. The promise of being happy is so alluring that it cannot help but generate an interest in moving forward.

`The reality of being amid that pain story leaves most of us wondering whether the established world really has any clue as to what they are talking about. Being happy. Really? Glimpses will come at the oddest moments. The ebb and flow of your own incredible journey will take you to the edge of happiness sometimes and tease your senses. Just know we all have the right to be happy, and if that does not work, go outside and let the sun shine on your face. Remember what the sun and happiness feel like and incorporate that into your daily mantra. It also helps to be listening to Creedence Clearwater Revival. Plus, you get some interesting looks when you are singing and dancing down the street.

Bless your journey.

Spirit

Systematic return of the spirit
is shocking and rewarding to the mind.

Freeing negative forces
helps to reverse the direction
that destiny so completely had control over.

The will to venture
into unknown and new scenes
creates a new story of facing forward and acceptance.

A rock chip in the car windshield can stay permanently and not cause any other damage. Or it can widen into a crack and spread out in all directions, hindering the driver's vision. I was looking at a rock chip in my truck's windshield. A crack was slowly forming in the glass.

It reminded me of my life since Barb died. The rock chip was the brilliant way that she died. It exploded on impact and sent fine lines around its circumference, very quickly and with a powerful and surprising sound.

At first glance, we did not see the hole that it left. On the second glance, we discovered it was worse than we thought. Eventually, a serious crack formed in the glass in two directions. Some of us followed its southerly route until it ended at an edge and we could sigh with relief. Others of us followed the northerly route that has no end in sight. We aimlessly zigzag, hoping we do not go crazy watching it unfold.

Some chips can be repaired, but the problem is still there. Or you can replace the entire windshield and start over as though it never happened. You will always know the windshield was broken and it was simply cleaned up. I do not know if I am going to get my chip fixed. After all, it reminds me of things I may not necessarily want to forget.

So Much Time

I spent so much time with you,
and now it is just changing.
You are in my thoughts.
You are in my light.
You are in my every second.

Letting go and progressing is not what
I thought I would ever do.

Without you, I knew I could not make it.
I could not function.
I would not be.

But realization of our life proceeding
has taken over.
Allowing me to carry you
and communicate.
Knowing life is more than the past
but also the future.

You and I will never really be apart.
Forever bonded, forever smart
to the universal nature of continuing on the road
to the changing story.

Chapter 10—Out of the Cave

The second Father's Day after Barb's death brought with it the realization that, for the first time, I didn't try to hide on a holiday. Until then, every holiday had been a painful reminder that the outside world was allowed to continue while I protected myself by not participating. I didn't pretend to understand what had happened over the last year and a half. People sometimes say time stands still. In my case it seemed as though time had disappeared. I honestly don't remember a lot of it. It does not seem possible that I had become what I call a *momdad* and had learned to live again, to work again, to feel, to find myself, and to write, all while in that fog of uncertainty. But it happened.

I discovered I was building the foundation for the future, becoming someone I liked, and taking the role of "father" back. My elder daughter told me she was glad to see me back again and to be able to talk with me like we had before. Honestly, I think I was always there somewhere, but the new me, the one I see in the mirror, really was a combination of old and new. The difference was that I survived and had created a goal-oriented person who is in control of his future.

Do not worry. I know the reality of that statement, but it sounds good and feels right to say it. I now incorporate the strengths of the past with the rights of the future. I am now present in my kids' lives and can be the father that Barb always knew I could be. I will make mistakes along the way, but I will not be in the cave anymore. Only sunshine for me, Baby.

The lesson learned here is that the fog will lift, the cave does open to the sunshine, and time will move forward with or without you. The moment will come when you will realize that rejoining the race brings with it the love that was there all along. After your protective timeout, you can come back whenever you want and reconnect.

Father's Day 2010 was a perfect time for me to allow a holiday to be important again. It was my coming-out party, allowing me to throw away the word *momdad* and proudly accept *dad* in its place.

Chapter 10 — Out of the Cave

Remember

Remember when walking meant you had to move?
Remember when the light went out of your eyes?
Remember when sinking into the fog was your best of days?
Remember when tears were your best friend,
and yelling at God was the alternative to blaming
yourself for everything?
Remember the sun did not shine anymore,
and the sound of rain dulled your senses?

Looking back is easy,
when you are facing forward.
Sensing that being one again with yourself,
finding love at the most opportune time,
releasing yourself to the fate
that happiness can and will be obtained.
What, then, is to be drawn
from the before and after?

Was it necessary?
Was it a lesson?
Did you invite it in,
or did you just live?

Answers are a dime a dozen.
Response is what matters.

Think.
Find.
Feel.
Be open.
Sense the purpose of all life.
Remember yourself.

Chapter 11

Into the Parade

*Offers of new awarenesses light forth as you
awaken back into your life.
What you believed was gone is Love,
bubbling from a new perspective.
~ Archangel Raphael*

I joined the local Rotary Club in my town because I saw the need to get myself into and reconnect with the community and the world. One of the big things the club does every year is the Fourth of July parade. There are 150 different entries that include floats, bands, politicians, and so on. There are also horses. Guess what I was given the responsibility for? Yep, horse entries. I have always loved horses, and as a kid I wanted to raise wild mustangs, so this assignment was no problem. Different staging areas throughout the neighborhoods are used to organize the groups in the parade. When the time comes, they are directed down a street to where they funnel, along with other groups coming from different areas, into the parade. It is controlled confusion at its best, but in the end, it all seems to come together.

At one point during this madness, I had a flash of intuition that our lives sometimes feel like the parade organizing. We are all being directed down certain paths and funneled onto the stage, although we don't necessarily know what is along the route. Sometimes people are throwing candy in celebration. Sometimes roadblocks prevent turning in the direction you want to go. Noise excites and confuses at the same time. Horse groups get antsy at the slightest provocation. Some people are in control, and others just follow directions.

Some people turn down a one-way street going the wrong way, and others stop and block traffic. There are also moments of whimsy and executive decision-making, such as when you are in control of the final two horse entries and suddenly realize the front of the parade is turning the corner of the street you are standing on after its three mile journey and coming in your direction. And you haven't had the remaining horses and their young riders even get in line to start their journey in the parade. Do you panic? Run the other way? Tell someone it's every man for himself? No. You very quickly send the horses down the street ahead of the oncoming parade and wave good-bye to the kids you just spent four hours

Chapter 11 — Into the Parade

with, knowing they are going to be inserted into a parade and be given experiences they will remember the rest of their lives. Then you get out of the road so you do not get run over by the precision motorcycle group weaving around the street.

I'm reminded of a saying from the movie, Forrest Gump, about how life is like a box of chocolates, with its unexpected surprises. I like the thought of inserting myself into the parade route and onto the stage of life. I won't know what will be around the corner until I get there. I will risk the momentarily stepping in horse manure in order to be fully alive and receive the candy being thrown at me. Barb will be waving from the sidewalk, and I will wave back, knowing I have her full support to march into whatever is ahead.

One Step

It only takes one step to move ahead,
to take you out of the whirl of emotions that you are in,
to set your sights on the distant shore,
to let yourself expand and fulfill your right.

It takes only a step.

One step for you,
one step for those around you,
one step for life.

It takes only a step.

Chapter 11 — Into the Parade

What is a perfect love? Is there such a thing? Does it require anything special to hold on to it? What does it feel like, and can that feeling be maintained for a lifetime? Of course, I do not have the answers, but as usual I have my opinions. I think there are so many kinds of love that a perfect love to me is one that I needed at a particular point in life.

For instance, having been married for so long, Barb's love for me was perfect. It provided a base, security, a great family, and, most important, a feeling of belonging. Were things perfect? Well, probably not, but I would imagine we could all say that. It was a "perfect" love for me in the cosmic sense of things. When you lose that perfect love, you find yourself asking whether you will ever be able to find the glove that will fit so well again. Then it dawns on you that you have the rest of your life to fill. So you start looking, even though it might only be subconsciously. After all, you found the "perfect love" once; why not again?

The problem is the definition of *perfect*. I think it can be confusing and unnecessary to expect perfection. I think humans want to put labels on things, which is why we are always looking for perfection. Why not just expect a relationship to be perfect for the moment, and if it is not perfect at some point in the future, so be it? If you are really waiting for perfection, then you might miss something that could have been important for your growth. You could also be transferring your definition onto some unsuspecting soul who wants nothing more than to be loved. Life is too short for what I call the "second life" to be hung up on comparisons to your past. Of course, mistakes will be made. Pain will definitely be present. But allowing yourself to be open to the possibilities of life in the long run will only bring the realization that there is life after death.

So what I suggest is to allow yourself to take the chance and use your "second life" to search, enjoy, and just be who you need to be. In other words, be perfect to yourself.

Chapter 11 — Into the Parade

Being at Peace

The call of the bird at night,
the lone star in the sky,
require so little,
to hear and see.

The dog barks with no one yelling,
the light shines in the face of the walker.
Be still and use the senses.

The rustle of the leaves under the feet,
the garage door opening and closing,
without a care of the fast-paced world.
Enter the space that is inside of you.

Expect nothing.
Sense everything.
Feel the love within yourself.
Being at peace, no matter where you are,
is a gift you deserve.

Chapter 12

Unexpected Paths

A journey of steps felt from the heart brings unexpected viewpoints to unravel hidden expectations to Divine awarenesses.
~ Archangel Raphael

As I headed out of town with my younger daughter, who is a basketball player on an Amateur Athletic Union team, I realized how different things are for the two of us compared to a year and half ago. Back then, we would never have been involved in making this happen for her in playing for a traveling team that plays all over the West Coast. It wasn't that we did not want to back her in this endeavor; it was more that when Barb was alive, we had diffcrent priorities and time constraints that would have made it impossible to make it happen. When she died, those constraints went out the window like a rush of air leaving a balloon.

That my daughter and I now had time on our side to use as we wished suddenly became painfully obvious. Because we are both sports oriented, supporting her desire to pursue playing at a higher level of girls basketball and trying to get her noticed by college coaches at these huge West Coast tournaments were easy.

I think we all find we have time on our hands we never thought conceivable compared to when our spouses were alive. It is an interesting phenomenon. Where does the time really come from? And when you have many kids like we had and could never support this kind of thing for the older kids, it does make it a little awkward when your youngest gets all the attention now that mom has died. The flip side is that my daughter and I have had bonding time during an unbelievable period in both of our lives. Imagine two weeks on the road with a teenage girl, driving all over California, going to events that could impact her future. No pressure there. Good thing I am so laid back and have always told her to just have fun. If it didn't go well, we were going to have one heck of a long drive back from San Diego. What an ironic twist of fate, that it took a death to bring us so close.

Life is unfair sometimes, but I would not give up this time with my daughter. I think if I could turn back the clock, I would, of course, have kept Barb here on this earth and at the same time would have developed this strong bond with my daughter. It is too bad we cannot always have everything we want. That day, I settled for three-pointers from my daughter for her mom.

Peace Blanket

Can you have a blanket made for peace,
woven with care,
held together with love,
protecting the souls that come together,
who need it the most?

Protecting the dreams,
warming the heart,
beating in its all-consuming
sense of security.

You are my peace blanket.
Protecting me from harm,
loving me with your warmth,
weaving me into something I always wanted to be,
and was just waiting for gentle weaver's hands,
to release the magic that was always there.

Chapter 12—Unexpected Paths

I learned some important lessons while on the road:

1. Five-hour energy drinks only last three.
2. Forgetting what city you are in when you have been on the road for two weeks is easy.
3. You can squeeze ten basketball players into your van if necessary. But why would you want to?
4. Realizing you are standing in front of a hotel that you stayed in on your honeymoon is surprising.
5. Teenage girl basketball players talk about things you do not want to hear, eat constantly, and have the most interesting smells, especially when traveling all day after a game.
6. Unknown and unusual things that may need to be carefully removed or beat with a stick mysteriously materialize in your car.
7. After seventeen hours on the road with your daughter, prying your fingers from the steering wheel is not easy.
8. Coming home to Northwest Oregon trees can bring tears to your eyes.

9. If you ever see another In-N-Out Burger, you may shoot yourself.
10. Just because you are tired does not mean your memories over the past year and a half go away. They follow you.
11. Having your daughter drive at high speeds on major freeways can make your connection to your maker exceptionally strong.
12. Showers in hotels never really work, and what is up with the coffee in the room?

When you look at a trip like the one I described from a larger perspective, you realize people are typically nice, you do things for the ones you love, girls travel well in packs, and your guardian angel is watching over you and rooting for the home team.

Thanks, Barb.

Chapter 12—Unexpected Paths

Companion

My constant companion,
is the thought, "What now?"

It goes with me whereever I go,
speaks gently to my listening heart,
finds me at the oddest moments,
and rejoices with me when it seems right.

Seen by itself,
it has no power.
Joined with my spirit,
we move together.

I seek its companionship,
knowing it has strength
to guide me on my journey,
even if I fail to recognize its wisdom.

Those weeks of traveling with my daughter were a giant leap in my transformation into duel parenthood. What I mean is I took on a very uncomfortable role that would have been Barb's realm. I feel I have entered into "the world of the female." Yes, I took my younger daughter to have her ears pierced. Not only did I step into a world I do not understand, but the pictures on the piercing shop's walls of where piercings can go were also quite overwhelming. I had no idea they could put metal in those places. It was like walking into a dream, with flowing water, artwork, and big couches. I know what you are thinking: *Man up and take it for the team.* I did, and it was just one more step on the journey of becoming the "super dad." I think I need some air.

Oh, and my daughter? She looked beautiful.

Chapter 12 — Unexpected Paths

The Burden

The relationship you had,
blended so well together,
created a bond
of not being separated.

You thought together,
with everything as one.
The energy melted into a cohesive strength
that was needed.

Now that they are gone,
you have a separate life.
You think as one because you have to.

No longer relying on each other to decide,
you enter a place of uncertainty.
You might be afraid to move ahead
to make a life of decisions.

Know in your heart
that your loved one is there,
helping you to carry the burden.

Brand, spanking-new babies are so tiny and soft that they cannot help but melt you into memories long forgotten. On our way to Los Angeles for basketball, my younger daughter and I went to Vegas to visit my older daughter, my nephew, and the family who just brought home their new baby, Elizabeth. My nephew and his wife parallel my own early story in a way that registers deeply within me. We both lost our firstborn sons. Our son, Joshua, had a heart problem and died at ten days old from complications in surgery. Their son, Joseph, died at birth from complications in delivery.

We went through similar angst during the following pregnancy with the second child. In the back of my mind was that nagging concern regarding whether everything would be okay the second time around. You go through the whole pregnancy with hope and faith. When the time comes, and the new baby enters into the world, you hear the nurse say the baby is breathing and has all his or her fingers and toes, and you finally breathe. You do not realize you had, in a sense, been holding your breath for the past nine months. I remember when Barb and I pulled off the side of the road after leaving the hospital and just took the time to be the new family, to look at the miracle all wrapped up like a cocoon, and to just breathe and cry.

Life gives us second chances after what would seem to be insurmountable losses. What we do with those second chances is entirely up to us. Beautiful new babies, second lives, new jobs, or new relationships are adventures. I believe they are all placed along our paths for a reason, and if we just learn to breathe again, we will utilize them to the fullest.

Scents

Scents of a time gone by,
recorded in the subconscious,
retrieving the memories,
when the time is right.

Flashes of what is past,
connected to what is present,
reminds the soul
to not forget.

Bring the flashes with you,
cherish the scene,
by how it makes you feel,
and do not forget the others.

Contained within those links
is the understanding
that the past and the present
are the avenue to who you are.

Chapter 13

Taking Stock

A journey inwards allows you to grow your light, creating a greater surface for you to Love. By being active in building your light, doors of sharing open, allowing Love's dynamic flow.
~ Archangel Raphael

Reflecting on a journey can sometimes bring insight about something you might have thought was a random act of the universe. When I started writing, I did not intend it to be for an audience, but we know how life can send us down new paths. For some reason, after nearly two years, I had a sudden urge to find out who I was then and to see if I could extrapolate meaning out of the journey, so I decided to go back to my early writings and actually read them.

I am still surprised I was hit over the head and inspired to write poetry. At a time when I could hardly walk, having that kind of extraordinary experience to me was a miracle. It suddenly opened my mind again and, most important, opened the door to my crushed spirit. Since then, I have met folks who were also inspired after the death of a spouse to do something that was out of character. I wonder if, when you are at your lowest depths of grief, God throws out a life raft for you to grab on to and then says, "Row."

To think we are watched over and will be given the opportunity to save ourselves is fascinating to me. I did start rowing, although I felt like I was not moving very fast. I slowly started to feel my physical body again because, for a long time, all I felt was numbness. This led to taking the first steps in walking farther and farther. I liken it to walking up a long flight of stairs that never seem to end, and then, all of a sudden, you are standing at the top and on flat ground.

I came to realize walking and riding my bike brought me from the place I honestly did not think I would come out of. I am convinced most folks reach a point where they are physically, emotionally, and spiritually at a crossroads and have to decide whether they are going to survive and move forward. What I learned was that, if you know someone in that situation, you can only encourage them. Keep in mind not all of us choose to move on. I learned as one part of your life gets unbalanced, it has a huge impact on all facets of your life.

Chapter 13 — Taking Stock

A death can have an impact on your beliefs, job, and relationships and can really mess up your physical and emotional body. It is like a spiral down the rabbit hole to hang out with Alice. If anyone ever tells you to hide your emotions, throw something at him or her. You know the old saying, "Guys do not cry." That is the biggest fallacy ever. Pain is pain, and unless you let it out, you will destroy yourself. So I tell you here that I am a proponent of releasing that unbelievable amount of grief. Otherwise, it will build up like steam in a teakettle until it is vented out as rage and sadness.

Expressing that grief probably did more than anything else to move me on the recovery path. Eventually those moments of madness diminish in intensity and become manageable. I discovered getting caught up in your own grief is fairly easy, and that you can easily leave your family members at the curb. You need to circle back and pick them up because, after all, they lost someone too. Then it becomes a joint venture in survival. It will have its ups and downs, but each and every person will travel on his or her own journey, in his or her own time, and will cross your path from time to time.

Finding me was a surprise also. Realizing I could smile again, have passion, love, return to improve in my job, start cooking, meet great people, take care of the dog, write, and have plans for the future were truly eye opening for me. "Normal" shifted so much that I decided in my second life that "normal" would be and look different. Advice from folks became commonplace, but ultimately going with my heart proved to be the best direction. You will find your own path that will lead you out of the fog. Trust in yourself to make the right decisions and to connect the dots. My passion was to listen to what was going on around me, connect the dots, and follow the path created. It continues today, and I am so thankful for the journey.

I believe that, personally, I have become closer to the source. Death, grief, and the fog could very easily push you in an opposite direction; but in my case, because of inspired writing, I became closer. I discarded blame, and forgiveness became my friend. Loneliness is a hurdle you have to face and overcome. I do not have any suggestions on overcoming loneliness because I believe we all will figure out how much loneliness we are willing to put up with and when it is time to do something about it. It is all good and perfect. Reflection is good because it shows you where you have come from, and you can compare that to what you are now.

Coming to grips with what happened and realizing that it means that you are, indeed, on a road that is real and beneficial to your ongoing life, means that you are paying attention. That is the ultimate lesson of the journey. If you are aware and paying attention, then you will see the different possibilities.

After doing this review, I can truly say with certainty, I have come a long way, Baby. I wish for you the same insight. If not now, then soon.

The Gift

Singled out,
to receive the gift.
Humbly accepted,
and willing to give out.

The gift of life.
The gift of love.
The gift of truth.
The gift of forgiveness.

Together with purpose,
given with intent,
brings reward to the spirit,
and purpose to the man.

Chapter 13—Taking Stock

Walking a tightrope without a net, with no protection, and only the hope of success and the risk of failure would seem, at first glance, to be stupid. I do not need to tell you what failure would mean. Families provide a net, as well as work, passion, love, and exercise. However, sometimes not having a net can provide you with the most profound growth experiences, especially when you are trying to survive the death of a loved one.

Recently, I was trying to decide if I should stop writing. You guessed it. These writings have been my safety net, and I thought maybe I should step out on the rope without a net. I asked for input from friends, and the consensus was that I should continue. I have been thinking for quite a while that I wanted to put this into some form of book format. To be honest, I could not mentally see a finished product, so I put it on hold. While walking and talking to myself and to Barb, the whole format picture came to me. Now I know how it is supposed to look, and all I have to do is make it happen. One of the most profound moments in the death of my spouse was, for me, to tell Barb it was okay to go. That was truly another moment of walking out on the tightrope without a net.

Eternally

Woven eternally,
within the framework of mankind,
is the love that can save
or the love that can blind.

Many times history has proven
that quests are taken,
for the love that can save
or the love that can blind.

Knowing which path to take,
at any point in time,
reflects the true spirit
of whether you will
be saved by love
or blinded by love.

Chapter 13—Taking Stock

Sometimes the most mundane activities provide insight. Getting my car washed the other day reminded me of my life. Like my car being pulled through the car wash, I am being pulled through space, and I get glimpses of the outside through all the hyperactivity going on around me. Coming through any death in a family can put you into that car-wash space. You are surrounded by all the noise and arms reaching out for you while being flooded by a deluge of water.

If you can relax just a little and try to look out through that fog, you will see something remarkable. Among the chaotic activities is a sparkling picture of what can and will be. You realize there is a world out there that can be beautiful and rewarding, and then you break out of the car wash into reality. I love it when these flashes of inspiration take hold. Continuing with that theme, while I was reworking my writings into the book version, one requirement I had was that I had to actually read what I had written at the beginning of my journey. What I have discovered is that it is not easy to see where I came from. However, that is what it is all about.

Peace

If peace had a feeling,
it would feel like a slight breeze
swirling around the body.

The coolness of the water
at the river's edge.

The look of a lover
when the time is right.

The warmth of the sun's rays
as they float through the tree
and gently rest on the arm.

Sitting in a meadow high in the mountains,
listening to nothing and everything at the same time.

Peace comes in many flavors,
moments, and sounds.

Being aware is only half of it.
Feeling peace is the completion.

Chapter 14

Surviving the Twists and Turns

Love rises forth to glue pieces that have been shattered.
Love lights the way for your soul to grow
to deeply experience the power of your now.
~ Archangel Raphael

When you are the survivor of death, it can be quite challenging to find your own way through all the land mines placed in front of you. Move to the left, the right, turn around, and run the other way are just some of the decisions you have to make to get through the minefield. But do you know what? When you are standing at the other end of the battlefield, looking back over your shoulder, you are more surprised than anyone that you have made it across. You initially thought there was no way you would ever survive the first land mine, let alone all the others.

Good for you! You survived. You made it.

What really struck me as more important than my own survival was looking to my right and left and seeing all of my kids standing next to me. They had survived and made it too. My God, what a miracle that was. People are on their own journeys of self-discovery created by their own faith, writing their own story, weaving their own love connection in with the rest of us. I am incredibly blessed to be part of this truly inspired family. Our journeys continue.

Thank You

For calling my name,
through time's eternal heartbeat.

For touching my soul,
with the love of the ages.

For pulling me back,
from the brink of confusion.

For directing my energy,
to a more important purpose.

Thank you for being you,
and for allowing me to find me,
within your love.

My best friend says that playing Frisbee golf is an accurate parallel to the journey through life. Without getting overly metaphysical about it, I find his statement well on point. You take this round rubber disc that comes in many weights, and you throw it. Typically, what happens is that the disc moves forward in some capacity. In my case, it usually doesn't go straight, or in the direction I intended when I let it go. However, it did move forward, which in life is sometimes a major accomplishment. It is fascinating to follow this disc around and see where it is going to end up and what drama is going to be created in any potential predicament. You can take in the sun and the surrounding scenery while wandering back and forth across the landscape. You can commune with others you meet along the way while looking for everyone's discs that flew out of bounds. You can also hang out with the folks who take it so seriously that failure is not in their vocabulary. Be one with the disc.

Playing Frisbee golf made me realize the following:

1. Moving forward is better than moving backward.
2. Strength and domination are not necessarily the best approaches.
3. Being in your body is helpful, but letting go is vital.

Chapter 14—Surviving the Twists and Turns

4. Friends can give great advice. You do not have to do it alone.
5. You will walk in dog poop, no matter what type of shoes you are wearing or what direction you go.
6. It does not take a rubber disc to create happiness. What you do with the disc and how you react to it are important.
7. When you see the disc fly over your head backward after you throw it, you smile, pick it up, and move forward again.

May the wind always be at your back, may your disc fly straight, and may you avoid all the dog poop.

Searching for Peace

Searching for peace
in every direction
can cause confusion
because it has a scattered nature.

Finding peace
within yourself
brings the energy center
to where it should be.

Having peace
is the link often lost
to the searching and finding
of the miracle within you.

Chapter 14—Surviving the Twists and Turns

Two trees standing side by side can still grow up and out, but they can also become intertwined, producing what would look like one tree. In some respects, it is true: They move together in the wind, swaying in unison. They break under the same stresses. They bend just right and show their intertwined beauty to the world. The earth feeds them both, allowing them to grow and reach out for those around them.

Illness can affect one or both trees, but because time does not stand still, one can become too ill to continue. One tree wakes up one spring morning and realizes that it is not touching the other tree anymore. Lost and lonely, it wants to disappear too, but it does not know where it would go. Frustrated and angry, it will not grow its leaves or stretch out in the sun to raise its limbs to the birds like it always has. Ready to give up, it raises itself to the sky and asks for help.

Just when things look like they are at the worst for the tree, it looks down and sees something poking out of the dirt. It senses excitement when it realizes that in the very same place where its former friend stood are many seedlings reaching up in the light toward his branches. The seedlings intertwine with its trunk and ask questions. Over time, they grow stronger and bigger, and even though no tree can replace his former friend, he knows that he has a purpose. His purpose is to show love, be loved, give wisdom when needed, and always remember his special friend with the grace and humility that a relationship like theirs has afforded.

Chapter 14—Surviving the Twists and Turns

Lights

White lights coming toward you,
red lights going that way.
Where are you going?
Are you running away?

Simple solutions
come with heavy prices.
Are you willing to give it up
to free yourself?

It is likely that finding yourself
among the different lights,
going in different directions,
can be considered the most
important lesson of your life.

Be one with the universe.
Go in the direction of the flow,
and stop fighting to save yourself.
Know that when you let go,
you will be carried.

Attending church to see my youngest son get baptized and confirmed was an important dot for me to connect in my own growth as a man who was lost, and who had lost a loved one. I had not been back to church since Barb's death, mainly, as I can only voice now, because the church was my wife. She was somehow involved all the time, and her spirit was so strong there. In retrospect, I think I consider it somewhat cowardly on my part for not facing that and being able to go back to church. On the other hand, I consider it my respect for Barb, her faith, and friendships by not interfering. Watching my son with his host family reminded me of times when our sizable family would sit in church and take up an entire pew. It was a good memory of family, hope, and looking to the future and renewal. Thanks to my son, I could somewhat put aside my fear and just remember that any church is a place of fellowship.

Chapter 14—Surviving the Twists and Turns

Another Time

Another time,
another moment,
forever lost
within the memories of the past.

Special thoughts,
brought back from the depths,
mingle with the present
to create a new memory.

Going forward,
memories mix old and new,
combining the forces,
creating the needed reawakening.

Chapter 15

The "Voice of Reason"

The world unfolds before your eyes, perfection at its core.
Humble servant, you are thus sending forth your light in Love.
~ Archangel Raphael

Now I am the voice of reason. This is not something I would have expected to hear from my son, but I accept it with humility and explain it to you.

One summer, my second-youngest son was riding a bike across the southern United States to raise awareness for water aid around the world. I got a text from him saying they were in trouble in the scorching heat, with twenty-five-mile-an-hour headwinds, and were being harassed by a local drunk while they were recuperating under a tree. As a parent, what would you think if you got that text? Right, I called to confirm their imminent death.

It turned out they were alive and just exhausted both physically and mentally. I asked where they were, and when my son told me, I realized it was in an area Barb and I had taken him to as a baby to visit her now-deceased aunt. Somehow, that one realization for him changed the whole picture of where he was. He could sense being there in the security of his mother's arms, and the environment suddenly became less menacing.

Is that not true for all of us in how we view life? Our perceptions about where we are and how we choose to see it are, indeed, everything. I like being the voice of reason, even though at the time, I thought I was just being the father figure.

Words

Words require little effort.
To say,
to feel,
and to mean.

It is the meaning
behind them,
that takes the effort
of interpretation.

What you say
might not be what you mean.
What you hear
might not be what you intended.

So clarify the meaning.
Say what you feel,
hear the real intent,
be genuine in the giving and taking,
and do not get lost in the confusion.

I think being alone and being lonely are two different things. I find that when I am "being alone," I am watching television at weird hours, thinking it is normal for a single person to think about such things as family pictures on the wall; wondering what happened to the little kids in those pictures, and thinking aloud that they all made it. Being alone and making a meal require little effort. I simply choose between an avocado or peanut butter. Neither one is necessarily a great choice, but who is going to complain? I could blame my wife for my being alone, but how is that going to help? She would just tell me to get over it and to do something constructive.

There are times in your life when being melancholy is a rite of passage. Being in this space allows me to write with more insight about myself and to walk long distances without paying attention to anything going on around me. That includes the curb I did not see, and where the heck did that beautiful sunset come from? You know what? Negative thinking enters our psyche because we allow it to. I am making the whole story up anyway. If I am alone and feeling bad about it, I can just as easily not be alone with myself and enjoy the experience. So, instead of blaming Barb for my being alone, I choose to enjoy the sunset until it is gone and eat peanut butter because I can.

Bon appetite!

The Trip

When a flower makes you cry
and a song breaks your heart,
regroup your thoughts,
take stock of how far you have traveled.

No trip is perfect.
Each journey has ups and downs,
reminding you
that you are never far from the bend in the road.

Staying on the road
is as important as you make it.
Going faster
will not make it safer.

Slow down
and enjoy the trip.
What comes tomorrow
may make all the difference.

Chapter 15 — The "Voice of Reason"

My target was the street corner approximately two miles from my house. Why should I have given a second thought to the place that was such a nemesis to me months after Barb died? At the time, this street corner was the halfway point of my self-inflicted route to recovery. I cannot stress how hard it was for me to get to that one spot on this big blue planet. It meant everything to me. All my life I have set goals for myself that were not only hard but also realistically achievable, producing rewards at the same time. This particular goal of reaching the halfway point of my walk was, I have to admit, probably the hardest goal I had ever set for myself. Not only did it require an extraordinary amount of willpower that I didn't think I had, but I also needed to overcome the negative self-talk of its being worthwhile.

I believe in setting goals, especially after losing someone in your life. You will fight it, but ultimately it will bring you through the maze and into the finding of who you really are. Now, when I walk by this former goal, I bow to its generosity in helping me on my path to a future that is goal oriented once again. I can look at the corner with fondness, knowing it did its part in my story.

Street Corner Sobriety

Reaching a place
that in days past required such strength
is sobering in its impact.

Realizing that you can come so far,
and fight off the demons that inflate their value,
and at the same time conquering the need to shrink.

Open up the possibilities
to begin life anew,
with the conviction of the future
strapped to your back.

Chapter 15 — The "Voice of Reason"

Have you ever prayed, wondered, meditated, wished, hoped, or just said something out loud, and it was answered before you finished saying it? I am always testing Barb and those others who have gone on to show me a sign that I am on the right path. Being a visual type of person, I like to see these signs. Being a "smart aleck" sometimes and considering my sense of humor, I have no trouble challenging the spirit world. One day, I was in need of a sign, and found a beautiful clear agate on the beach. I know they are not common, because I have spent so much time on the beach. Being that I have an affinity for the number nine, I challenged Barb, and anyone listening to show me nine of these rocks on the way back to my car. I had a lot of faith that I would end up with exactly nine, but because there are no rules when it comes to spirit, I thought it would be fun to see how it played out. Well, you can guess what happened. I found nine clear agates; my faith was validated, challenged, accepted, and brought home.

You would think I would learn that challenges are not necessary and that love crosses all boundaries. Perception is everything when it comes to miracles. I know I will keep asking and looking, and when it is my turn to go, Barb and I will have quite a conversation and laugh about how I kept trying to challenge her and the others. We are all looking for a connection that gives feedback through validation. I believe attempting to communicate with love, respect, and intention is a form of leading with your heart and keeping an open mind to the possibilities within the human potential. Without the belief of this potential, hope, and wonder, we are left with only the cold proof of man-made science. I find that unacceptable and boring at the same time.

Chapter 15 — The "Voice of Reason"

You Are With Me

How do I know you are with me?
Are you holding my hand?
Are you putting your arm around me?
Are you whispering in my ear?

I see your face in the stars.
The brilliance of your soul
shines bright.

I hear your voice in the breeze.
A welcome breath against my ear.

I feel your presence in the wind,
surrounded by the love
of nature's commitment.

You are everywhere and nowhere,
on the outside and in between,
completely and forever,
always there to answer.

Chapter 16

Those Little Moments

Light and Love swirl together, celebrating joys of togetherness.
Gratitude is the gift of receiving the joy of your Love.
~ Archangel Raphael

Trust me; I have seen fall colors before. I have seen light come through the trees and watched branches sway gently in the wind. But where do all these colors come from? What about the light, the warmth of the sun, and the wind in the trees? I am not talking about the science behind these things but those moments in which the world amazes me.

The only way I can describe what is going on with my senses is to compare it to what I assume being born is like, coming out would have to be brilliant in the colors, sounds, touches, smells, and tastes we experience. If those moments could speak, I would think they would be some of those "wow" moments.

I think the term of being *reborn* has been overused, but it really does describe the sights, sounds, and feelings when I suddenly find enough time has transpired to be able to step into the world. This life has been there the whole time I have been gone. I really do like "wow" moments and always find them fascinating. They are beyond my words of explanation. To feel alive with purpose and intention is not something that I thought would be possible again. I realize that profound moments are God's way of saying "Wake up."

I have to go; I have a rainbow to chase.

Transformation

*Formed by grief,
healed by love,
transformed by spirit.*

*Written without writing,
spoken without speaking,
felt without feelings,
known without knowing.*

*Transformation by divine love,
into second life.
You are never alone.
Reach out, and write, speak, feel, and know.*

Turning points in one's life can take many forms. You can have an experience so profound that you will never look at things the same way again. You can get angry at your deceased spouse, and get a response that tells you she is listening. You can have love in your life that surprises you because you were not sure that you would feel it again. Or you could go looking for clam chowder on the Oregon coast and not find it anywhere.

All I wanted was New England clam chowder. I drove in the pitch-black night and pouring rain, not really understanding why. I ended up at a state park with no name, and as I entered the parking lot, I realized I had entered some sort of calm in the storm. The rain had stopped, and the sky was so clear that the stars were the most brilliant jewels in the sky I'd ever seen. Venus glowed, and the Big Dipper was bright, hanging low near the horizon. I actually felt like I could reach out and touch the heavens. I heard the breeze and the surf as one source of sound like a steady and strong heartbeat. Funny thing: The next day on the way home, I noticed clam chowder everywhere. Isn't that interesting?

To me, turning points are ones that take you away from your planned goal and lead you to an unexpected and profound

Chapter 16 — Those Little Moments

spiritual uplift. Whether you pay attention is your choice. I am guessing experiences like this do not happen every day.

Synchronicity

One thing happens,
another comes along.
Without much thought,
they both tie together.

Things happen for a reason,
not by chance.
There are no coincidences,
if you just relax and look.

Pay attention to what is happening around
and through you.
Do not let anyone tell you
that synchronicity is a dream.

Chapter 16—Those Little Moments

Forty years from now, I want to look Barb in the eyes and say, "Thank you for the journey." Sometimes, I truly wonder what I am going to write about. I occasionally throw the question out to the universe and see what happens. That is the interesting thing about inspired thought. You never know when it is going to hit you and who might be sending you the message. That line came to me with intention and full-body goose bumps. That is when I pay attention.

Of course, these inspirational pulses that arrive unexpectedly always seem to have double meanings. Being a reporter-minded person, I decided to analyze it. It could mean that when it is my time to go, I get to look Barbara in the face and thank her for saving my butt, hooking me up with incredible friends, and telling me to wake up and pay attention to the incredible opportunities. It could mean thanking my second life love for the patience of seeing the journey through with me. I would be overwhelmingly humbled to think that I was able to be connected to two beautiful souls. To know I lived such a profound and rewarding life, including such great kids who allowed me to be their father.

Of course, I am just ad-libbing here, but if you have lost someone in your life, you need to be told it is okay to plan for the future. You survived for a reason, and being able to honor your past and your future with thanksgiving is what you need to give yourself as your present.

Chapter 16 — Those Little Moments

Eagle

I heard the eagle from a distance,
never seeing its flight,
in swooping over the river,
retrieving fish for its family.

Faith in knowing the eagle is there,
is enough for the moment.
Realizing I do not need to see things,
to believe in their existence.

Without faith,
there is the need for proof.
Imagination only requires
the faith to believe so hard,
that you know its existence is real.

As the holidays approached for the second time since Barb's death, I anticipated trouble. We weren't waiting for it, but emotions can be like someone peeking around the corner at you. They sneak up when you least expect it and remind you of things you hope you could hide a little longer. Almost two years after Barb's death, although there is some angst, sadness, and a little anger, I also have a sense of peace and knowing. The knowing is about my understanding, that when I first started writing this, I did not care if anyone was reading. That was not what it was about. It was all about putting feelings to paper and finding out it helped in healing and moving forward, one step at a time.

As time went on, I realized that folks were reading what I was writing, and my writing took on some form of responsibility. Hearing from people who voiced similar experiences made me realize we are not alone, even if we think we are. Healing continued for me in knowing that touching other people through writing was my way of rising from the ashes. Finally, knowing the holidays are gentler now because of the journey I have taken makes me want to thank all those who listened and cared and were part of the healing team.

Thank you all for your friendship, love, and input into this humble soul.

Past and Future

Swinging between past and future
can sometimes affect your equilibrium.
Focusing on one only
can affect your wholeness.

Being within both
does require the focus
to grasp that life is not
made up of one or the other.

You can be in the past and the future,
allowing both to guide you
on the road to discovery.

Chapter 17

Connecting and Reflecting

*You are you, fulfilling the destiny to know Love wholly.
All experiences weave light to illuminate
the eternal oneness of Love's embrace.*
~ Archangel Raphael

I realize I spend a lot of my time waiting for something to happen. Since Barb died, my life has been made up of connecting the dots with the hope that they will lead somewhere. I am so convinced they will continue to guide me that I sometimes forget that it is not necessary to be like the kid on Christmas morning, patiently waiting to see what is going to be in the box. Just allowing things to happen, noticing them, and reacting to them would probably be less stressful. Instead, I am always speculating what might happen next.

The holidays are still hard for me personally, even though I put on a great mask to show that everything is fine. The reality is this will probably be the case for years to come. I guess by waiting for something to happen, it is my way to cope and push the negative stuff way deep down inside and to hide it under my grandmother's trunk in the basement. By waiting for something to happen, I keep the possibilities of the future and the childlike qualities alive within me. In a way, we are all waiting for something to happen. We live our lives, raise our families, and rejoice that it is all leading somewhere special.

Mist

Seeing through the mist of perception,
fighting hard to sort out the hidden meaning.

What you get is a world
that fits your idea,
not necessarily the world around you.

It is never easy to sort through the fog,
for what is real and what is not.

In the end,
it is what you make of everything you do and apply.

After a loss, reflection is a great way to determine whether, in your mind, you are advancing in some capacity through the process called grief. So I looked at what I didn't do anymore:

1. Walk slowly in a stooped position. It is more painful to walk that way.
2. Leave the dishes for the kids to do. We all know who is going to do them anyway.
3. Pay attention to any political campaign. Things do not really change, anyway. If you think they do, then run for something and find out.
4. Think the world should have stopped turning when Barb died. It did not, and it would not have been fair to the rest of you if it did.
5. Hope they will do the right thing. They might not, but if I do, then that is all that matters.
6. Wonder if I should tell someone what I really think. If what you share is important enough, who knows? You might save a life.
7. Think that I am not being listened too. Trust me. You are being listened to. The real question is, how are you interpreting the feedback you receive?

Chapter 17—Connecting and Reflecting

8. Rake up all the leaves after they fall. Blowing leaves to the side of the yard while rationalizing it as mulch is the ultimate protest to do the thing in the same way for so many years. After all, don't leaves fall in the forest? You do not see anyone raking those leaves up.

9. Think that love will never find me again. There are so many forms of love that we never knew existed. Be open to different delivery methods, and you know that love will find you and that it will be perfect for you.

10. Think that writing silly, fluffy, deeply felt views is something you would never catch me doing.

Happiness

Happiness is a state of grace.
Fleeting for some,
controlled by others.

Never be satisfied
to accept anything less
than the desired outcome.

Reach inside and pull it from the depths.
Expect it for yourself,
retreating only when your spirit
requires it.

Magic happens when you decide
that happiness is a right of being human,
and face its consequences head on.

Chapter 17 — Connecting and Reflecting

Reflective thinking can at times be a burden. If you are always thinking at a deeper level and trying to figure out where you fit within the framework of life, you may just miss the perfection of simplicity. As the calendar approached the two-year anniversary of Barb's death, I knew I had done a lot of reflecting through writing and paying attention to this wonderful and, yes, painful journey. I wonder if, when you lose someone, you can fall into the trap of being overly profound and miss what is staring you in the face.

His name is Jack, and as I write this he has just come in from the backyard covered in mud. My yard during the winter in the Northwest becomes a mud bog. Jack is a pure white West Highland terrier. When he decides the neighborhood cat needs to be chased through our mud bog, he even attempts the ten-point slide tackle, and there is no stopping him. So, as my black dog sits in front of me, looking up at me with those innocent eyes, I cannot help but think that Jack is the perfection of simplicity. Thinking deeply is not necessarily helpful at moments like this. Seeing me laughing reflected in his eyes meant just as much.

Here is a reflective thought for you: I see a cleansing in someone's future and a restoration to wholeness.

Being Lost

In being lost, you can see the stars more clearly,
and contemplate who you are.

Being lost makes walking quieter,
and loneliness easier to take.

Being lost creates a void,
into which you can push your thoughts.

Being lost makes things seem less important,
and gives meaning to the source of life.

Lost in thought.
Lost your mind.
Lost your way.
Lost between night and day.

It only remains to be seen,
if the importance is being lost,
or that the lost needs to be found.

Chapter 17—Connecting and Reflecting

When it comes to your own existence here on earth, how do you know you are doing the right thing? Is it faith alone or a feeling? Do you rely on your intuition, or do you allow other people to make decisions for you? I know this may seem deep right now, especially at Christmas time. For me it is the perfect time to reflect on what I am doing, how I got here, and how I make choices. I believe I listen to the past, present, and future using intuition, feelings, verbal clues, and sometimes luck. I know one thing: In the awakening through death, I have become more open, and I have also become unwilling to continue what I was doing previously because it was the easiest path.

Even though I am the same person, I am also not the same person. I move forward in a different, but just as good a way, with intention and a love that I have never felt for myself. I know I am being watched over and guided by folks who want us to succeed. All of us have our own methods for doing the right thing. I wish you well and hope you realize that the right thing can be achieved by opening yourself up. Become aware of the different modalities being presented to you, and there truly is life after death.

Weight

Weighed down by the past,
free to fly with the future,
shaped by tomorrow,
with a foot in the door of yesterday.

Sensing a tie between it all,
unwilling to give up any,
the right of every human
resides within the juggling act.

Contained within the whole,
perfected by the pieces,
reaching out
to create the puzzle of life.

Chapter 17—Connecting and Reflecting

Being thankful should be the obvious choice for anyone. After all, it provides us the opportunity to remember someone special came into our lives and made a real difference in how we lived. I, for one, am so thankful to know that those in spirit cared enough to come and share their time here with me, to guide me when they thought it was appropriate, to pull me out of harm's way at times, and, most of all, to surround me with that special love that only they can exude. Being thankful does not seem like enough for that special gift. I believe passing the gift on is the ultimate responsibility for all of us, and a way for them to continue to help us share the gift. Thanks for coming, sharing, protecting, and helping us become the gift to those around us.

You Know Someone Loves You

You can feel it in your heart.
You can feel it in your bones.
You are not afraid to go away,
because you know that someone loves you.

It is a whole body experience,
to see them wherever you are.
Lose the noise,
listen to the soul,
because you know that someone loves you.

Time will not tell,
because it does not exist.
Be in the moment.
You know that someone loves you.

Peaceful reminder,
how good it can feel.
Knowledge is right,
because you know that someone loves you.

Chapter 18

The End and the Beginning

*Celebrate the cycles of the sunrise and the sunset,
renewing each breath to say hello to your now.
~ Archangel Raphael*

The cave was almost completely dark. Only a single candle that seemed never to melt provided light, spreading it in all directions. He could see a few feet ahead but was still confused about what might lie ahead. Others considered the risk and fear of what was in the darkness too great to risk entering the cave. After all, one may go in and never come back, and that would truly be sad for everyone involved.

The light from the single candle radiated with such clarity and intensity that he just knew he was on the right path. He always trusted his intuition but admitted he did not always follow it. He personally did not feel he had anything to lose. They tried to tell him not to go into the cave. Because of his stubbornness, he thought there had to be more to life than to be the person he had always been. He needed to see the cave. He truly believed he could not go on the same way he was.

He seemed to make friends with the candle, which apparently was helping him find his way out of the darkness, even if it did mean he was not conforming to the advice of those around him. He became so tired physically and mentally that he had to lie down and rest. Dreaming was not something he did often, but when the candle spoke to him, he was not sure if he was asleep or awake.

"You do not have to do it alone."

"What is that supposed to mean? Of course I have to do it alone. I am the only one here now," he said. He became angry that the candle had spoken and told him something that did not appear to make sense. He was not the type of person who never listened; he just felt so strongly about what he was doing, in spite of not being able to see the path.

No longer able to sleep, he chose to think about what he thought the candle had said. Not having to do it alone would mean he needed to ask one of his

Chapter 18 — The End and the Beginning

friends to come with him. Confused, he became frightened for the first time. He said a prayer.

"God grant me the wisdom to see who I really am, and to be who I should be. Help me on this journey to become what was intended through your guidance, and show me the way with help in finding peace in everything I do, joy in what I choose, and freedom and love all around me."

Another voice in the darkness said, "Look in your pocket."

The man reached into his pocket and felt another candle. Using the first candle, he lit this new wick.

"You are not alone," the voice said. "You now have two candles that shine together as one, illuminating the path you choose. You do not have to put out the first candle, as it will always act in unison with the second candle in guiding you on your path. Always be humble and know that your past is as brightly lit as your future. We go there together in the hopes that you remember where you came from, and realize you never have to do it alone. You will always be surrounded by the clarity and illumination of the joint flame within your heart. Go now, and follow the path together. Know that I will always stay with you when times are tough, protecting you and those that you love."

With tears of gratitude and without fear, he and the candles moved forward out of the other end of the cave and into the light of illumination.

My journey during the two years after Barb's death has been profound for me. I have survived the continuous onslaught of emotions, feelings, and general emotional roller coaster that accompanies the death of someone so close that you thought you were one body. I have been inspired all along this journey to do things I never thought I could do. Writing poetry, blogs, and books was surely not part of my vision for myself, prior to Barb's dying. Only through a series of what I called "inspired thought" and following the dots can I now see the bigger picture was larger, with very intentional consequences.

At the time, I could not necessarily make sense of it, but I was being guided to come out of the darkness. The darkness is what people go through when they have profound loss, and each and every one of us has to make the conscious decision to move through the darkness into the light. I had demanded that Barb

Chapter 18—The End and the Beginning

participate in my life, admitting I could not do it alone. I am not sure I thought the answers would come the way they did.

A friend once asked me, "When does the mourning ever end?" I realized it does not. It only changes. It changes to a more manageable and loving way to handle the grief. It only requires you to be open to the idea that your loved one's memory is a gift and that, as a gift, it should be treated with open arms and gratitude. I now know Barb continues to guide me, make me laugh, and inspire me to make something of my life. She was my candle, and when combined with the current love of my life, they have made a great team of which I am truly honored to be a part.

I will forever be grateful for the love that Barb showed me while alive and continues to show me in her death. I consider myself incredibly lucky to have two candles burning in my life. The end of the book is simply that. This is exactly the right timing to end a journey of discovery through death and life for me. It is not really the end, but a beginning, linking the first life with the second. One is not better than the other, only different. I cannot really see any farther into the darkness than you can, but I am willing to keep my past and future illuminated with love. I will enjoy the journey that is in front of me, knowing I am indeed not alone on the trip.

I understand one true and meaningful thought. Writing this book was a very important choice in my life. I emphasize *choice* because it has required me to reflect and know that all the decisions I have made on this journey have been my choices. Yes, I can tell you that the suggestions of others had an impact on these choices at times, including inspired input from Barbara Grace Russell. But one thing is clear to me: No amount of inspired input or suggestions from friends and family can influence someone if they are not ready to receive.

In my cave, praying for help was choice. Choosing to live, to die, to love, and to be loved in my life. Choosing to move forward or to stand still. Choosing the path to the left or the right. I chose to write this book and help heal myself with truth and pain in an effort to take one step at a time. My hope is that, by writing from the male perspective, I was able to show that feelings are not the sole purview of the feminine. In writing my story, I hope I was able to touch the heart that needed opening, and if even one person benefited from my journey, then the benefit was immeasurable.

To me, the butterfly effect is that you do one thing, which affects another. If you know someone who needs to read this story, then pass it on. You will be the butterfly. Bless you for your support of me and my journey and never give up. With gratitude and humbleness I move forward.

*With greater light the will to live flows stronger in all you are.
Reach out to create connections deeper than before.
~ Archangel Raphael*

Acknowledgments

I would like to thank all of those people in my life who encouraged me through the drama of the grieving process. I would like to dedicate this book first and foremost to Barbara Grace Russell, whose support and love over many years helped make me the person that I am today. Her life and death so profoundly affected so many lives, and she will be remembered with love and affection by her family and friends.

I would like to thank a couple of people who encouraged me to continue to connect the dots during the journey and really use my voice to help not only myself but others who have taken the same path. Thank you, Becky Shipman, for encouraging the voice of pain to come out and be heard. Thank you, Lynn St. Georges, for taking the initial steps to edit the ramblings of someone who didn't necessarily think that there was a voice. Thank you, Dave and Kellie Poulsen-Grill, for helping me understand that it was okay to love again and to see that in you. Thank you, Margie Boule, for taking the story of a broken, demanding man and seeing the grace of the universe within its telling in your column.

Gratitude goes out to Ardel Chisholm, our graphic designer from LincMedia Design, who, as usual, takes my thoughts for the cover and creates a design that fits my vision. And a big hug to my publisher, Sharon Lund of Sacred Life Publishers, and my editors, Wendy Jo Dymond and Lynette Smith, for their continued support and expertise in their areas.

Thanks have to go out to those who actually read the manuscript and gave feedback. Thank you, Elizabeth Roberts and Michael Krol. Steve Arndt, my longtime friend and mentor who wrote the foreword to this book, has my admiration; I am humbled that he took on the role. Special thanks go to my son Garrett Russell for taking the time to teach me to organize my writings in a more professionally accepted manner.

This journey would not have been possible without Micah, Betty, Garrett, Dale, Devon, and April. As my children, they provided me with inspiration and stories to be able to piece together the time frame that this book covers. I do not believe that I can ever show my appreciation to them for the love, patience, emotions, and support they provided and had to go through themselves over this same time. I never want to forget that death is

Acknowledgments

the journey of not just one person, but the whole team. So thank you for putting up with me during this time. Even though we went through so much as a family, I look at us now and see a profoundly strong group of individuals of whom I am so proud.

And finally, I could not have completed this book without the help of my current wife, Trisha Michael. Yes, there is life after death, and love can happen again. Because of Trisha's constant love for me and her encouragement, I have been able to see this project through to its completion. With her help as a channel for Archangel Raphael, I not only invited his input to each section of this book, but I am so honored that he was willing to provide such great words of wisdom, and tie together the progression of time and the various stages of the grief process with his insights.

May this book provide insight to those who read it and give heart to those in need now and in the future. Belief and hope are two reasons that there is a light at the end of the tunnel through the process of losing someone, and we all have the right to accept nothing less.

About the Author

Mike Russsell

Mike Russell was inspired to write this book with the help of his angelic wife, Barbara Russell. Through this unique collaboration of what first was poetry and then a blog, this project evolved into a book. With the help of Trisha Michael, he was able to ask for guidance from Archangel Raphael, who provided meaningful quotes that helped weave the timeframe of grief into a mosaic of a personal journey through the universal story of losing someone close.

Mike has worked as a banker and lender most of his adult life and has only recently been involved in many writing projects while participating in the growth of the T. Michael Healing Arts Clinic. He continues to help in getting the channeled messages of Archangel Raphael out through the various sources of publication and video.

For more information go to www.tmichaelhealingarts.com, where you will find many more messages and videos that can help you on your own journey through life's mysteries.

www.ingramcontent.com/pod-product-compliance
Lightning Source LLC
Chambersburg PA
CBHW050631300426
44112CB00012B/1744